W9-DEO-722

Political Parties in Israel

David M. Zohar

The Praeger Special Studies program—
utilizing the most modern and efficient book
production techniques and a selective
worldwide distribution network—makes
available to the academic, government, and
business communities significant, timely
research in U.S. and international economic, social, and political development.

Political Parties in Israel
The Evolution of Israeli Democracy

PRAEGER SPECIAL STUDIES IN INTERNATIONAL POLITICS AND GOVERNMENT

Praeger Publishers   New York   Washington   London

Library of Congress Cataloging in Publication Data

Zohar, David M
    Political parties in Israel.

    (Praeger special studies in international politics
and government)
    Bibliography: p.
    1. Political parties—Israel. I. Title.
JQ1825.P37Z64   329.9'5694   73-15201
ISBN 0-275-28814-5

JQ
1825
.P37
Z64
1974

PRAEGER PUBLISHERS
111 Fourth Avenue, New York, N.Y. 10003, U.S.A.
5, Cromwell Place, London SW7 2JL, England

Published in the United States of America in 1974
by Praeger Publishers, Inc.

All rights reserved

© 1974 by Praeger Publishers, Inc.

Printed in the United States of America

To My Parents

ALMA COLLEGE
MONTEITH LIBRARY
ALMA, MICHIGAN

This book is based on an M.A. thesis submitted to the Department of Civics and Politics at the University of Bombay, India, in 1972, and draws mainly upon existing secondary source publications in English and Hebrew, especially in updating to 1974. In addition, use has been made of primary Israeli material in Hebrew.

Although employed by the Israeli Ministry for Foreign Affairs, which kindly gave me permission to publish this book, I am solely responsible for all statements of fact and opinion presented, and the book neither contains material not generally obtainable by the public nor represents the Israeli government in any way.

I owe a debt of thanks to Dr. A. J. Dastur, Dr. R. Srinivasan, and the staff of the University of Bombay for their guidance and helpfulness; to my father, Lucien Harris of Jerusalem, and my colleague J. de Jonge of the Netherlands Consulate in Bombay, for their valuable criticism; and above all to my wife and two daughters, for their patience and support of this endeavor.

My thanks to all the distinguished scholars who so kindly gave permission for their works to be used.

Politics being a peculiarly sensitive subject, may I apologize in advance to any person, faction, group, party, or movement I may have misrepresented in any way in this book.

David M. Zohar
Los Angeles, 1974

CONTENTS

		Page
PREFACE		vii
LIST OF TABLES AND CHART		xii
LIST OF TERMS, ABBREVIATIONS, AND ACRONYMS		xiii
INTRODUCTION		xv

Chapter

1	ZIONISM	1

The Early History of Zionism ... 1
The Ideological Growth of Zionism ... 4
Notes ... 10

2	THE EMBRYO STATE: ITS INSTITUTIONS AND PARTIES	11

The Elected Assemblies ... 11
Independence: The Interim Period ... 16
Notes ... 18

3	POLITICAL DEVELOPMENT AFTER INDEPENDENCE	20

Notes ... 32

4	THE MAJOR POLITICAL BLOCS	34

The Labor Movement and Its Parties ... 36
  The History of the Israeli Labor Movement ... 37
  The Growth of the Labor Movement ... 42
  The Israel Labour Party ... 44
The Nationalist Parties ... 48
The Religious Parties ... 50
The Communists ... 54
Notes ... 56

Chapter   Page

5   KNESSET AND LOCAL ELECTIONS   58

      How Elections Are Held   58
      Electoral Reforms in 1973   63
         Local Government Elections   63
         Knesset Elections   64
      Fifty Years of Voting Trends (1920-70)   66
      The First Knesset Election after Independence   67
      Voting Patterns since Independence (1949-69)   69
      The Parties That Failed   74
      The Political Acculturation of Immigrants   75
      The Organized Electorate: Political Youth
         Movements and Villages   78
      The Kibbutz in Israeli Politics   80
      Voting Patterns of Israeli Minority Groups   81
      Notes   83

6   THE KNESSET--ISRAEL'S PARLIAMENT   85

      Candidate Selection   85
      The Parliamentary Party (Si'ah)   90
      The Power of the Knesset Member (Questions)   92
      Notes   94

7   GOVERNMENT BY COALITION   95

      Main Political Issues   95
      The Constitutional Problem   100
      Notes   102

8   POLITICAL FINANCE   103

      Where the Money Comes from   103
      Party Politics and the Prevention of Corruption
         in Government   106
      Notes   107

9   THE 1973 ELECTION YEAR   108

      Histadrut, Knesset, and Municipalities   108
      Postscript: Spring 1974   113
         The Knesset   113
         Electoral Reform   114
         The Cabinet   116
      Notes   116

	Page
CONCLUSION	117
Appendix	
A STATISTICAL APPENDIX	119
B COMPOSITION OF THE MARCH 1974 CABINET	130
C DOCUMENTS	131
D CHRONOLOGY	184
E THE NEW ISRAELI CABINET	187
SELECTED BIBLIOGRAPHY	191
ABOUT THE AUTHOR	195

LIST OF TABLES AND CHART

Table		Page
1	Composition of the Four Elected Assemblies	14
2	Composition of the People's Council	17
3	Composition of the People's Administration	17
4	The Political Spectrum	22
5	Political Attitudes in Israeli Parties	35
6	Israeli, British, and Indian Electoral Systems--A Theoretical Comparison	61
7	Contending Parties, First to Eighth Knesset	70
8	Average Vote Distribution to the Seventh Knesset, by Percentages	73
9	The Parties That Failed in the Fourth Knesset	75
10	Geographical Origin of Knesset Members	87
A.1	Knesset Election Results, 1949-65	119
A.2	Seventh Knesset Election Results--October 28, 1969, with State of Parties at the End of Sixth Knesset	120
A.3	Eighth Knesset Elections, December 31, 1973	121
A.4	Eighth Knesset Election: Breakdown by Townships	122
A.5	Histadrut Elections, 1956-73	124
A.6	Comparative Histadrut Party Strengths on a Geographic Basis, 1973	125
A.7	1973 Municipal Election Results (Major Cities)	126

Chart

	Fifty Years of Free Elections	128

LIST OF TERMS, ABBREVIATIONS, AND ACRONYMS

Ahdut Ha'avodah:	Unity of Labour Party
Asefat Hanivharim:	Assembly of the Elected; Jewish "parliament" during Mandate
BCE (Before Common Era)	B.C. (Before Christ)
CE (Common Era):	A.D. (Anno Domini)
Etzel (Irgun Zvai Leumi):	National Military Organisation
Gahal (Gush Herut-Liberalim):	Herut-Liberal Knesset bloc
Hagana:	Jewish Defence Force
Histadrut (Histadrut Haovdim Haklalit):	General Federation of Labour
Knesset:	Parliament
Lehi (Lohamei Herut Yisrael):	Israel Freedom Fighters
Likud Union:	Center-right coalition in the Knesset
Ma'arach:	Labour Alignment in the Knesset
Mafdal (Hamiflaga Hadatit Haleumit:	National Religious Party
Maki (Hamiflaga Hakomunistit Hayisraelit):	Israel Communist Party
Mapai (Mifleget Poalei Eretz Yisrael):	Israel Workers' Party
Mapam (Mifleget Hapoalim Hameuhedet):	United Workers' Party
Minhelet Ha'am:	People's Administration
Moetset Ha'am:	People's Council
Mops (Mifleget Poalim Sozialistit):	Socialist Workers' Party
Rafi (Reshimat Poalei Yisrael):	Israel Workers' List
Siach (Smol Yisraeli Hadash):	Israeli New Left
Si'ah:	Parliamentary Party
Sochnut (Hasochnut Hayehudit Leeretz Yisrael):	Jewish Agency for Palestine
Wizo:	Women's International Zionist Organisation

In order fully to understand modern Israel, one must begin with ancient Israel. Without a single exception, all Israeli parties and politicians relate themselves, their beliefs, actions, ideals, and motivations to a chrono-logically distant, but nonetheless real and vivid, epoch in Israel's history. The fact that in the very same territory, 3,000 years ago, their forefathers constituted an independent nation, culture, and society, which was to bequeath to the world that compendium of books known as the Bible, is for Israelis not a matter of long-dead history but a source of living identity. It is for this reason that an introduction to modern Israeli politics must begin with a sketch of ancient history.

Seen with the perspective of millennia, Asian history may be said to have had three major foci of development, located in West, South, and East Asia, respectively. Israel, India, and China have each given the world and posterity a wealth of tradition, art, learning, and insight, in the form of religious ideas and practices, legal systems, philosophies, and life patterns.

At the time when the Aryan peoples gradually gave their character to the lands south of the Himalayas, and the Chou dynasty succeeded the Shang in China, a small group of semitic tribes coalesced in West Asia, by the Mediterranean Sea.

The twelve tribes of Israel, descended according to tradition from the patriarchs--Abraham, Isaac, and Jacob--were a pastoral people who wandered with their sheep and cattle in search of pasture. Slowly they changed their occupation to that of the sedentary agriculturist, a transition that was to consolidate them as a nation. At an early point in their history, as recorded, the tribes came under Egyptian domination and were forcibly enslaved. Tradition relates that the Jews were compelled to build the pyramids of Egypt. After several generations of bondage they were able to escape from Egypt under the leadership of Moses, who led them back to their homeland, already known to them as "the Promised Land, the Land of Israel." At Mount Sinai the assembled people received the Ten Commandments and forged the mystical religious and national ties that ever since have held the Jewish nation of believers together.

Modern scholars hold that the tribes reentered the land in the middle of the 13th century BCE, early in the reign of the Egyptian Rameses II (1260-20 BCE). The tribal confederation eventually was replaced by a unified monarchy under King Saul. His successor, King David, established the capital in Jerusalem in 1000 BCE, where David's son, Solomon, built the great temple that was to become the focus and symbol of Jewish national independence and religious consciousness.

The prophets of the Jewish nation, called neviim, were men of vision who often left their families, vocations, and homes in order to preach the word of God, to speak for their conscience, and if necessary to challenge the powers that be. Israel's first "politically minded" personalities were such prophets as Isaiah and Jeremiah, who spoke not only on matters of heaven but also on matters of state; the latter suffering in the royal dungeon for his outspoken criticism of the King's foreign policy. The prophets of the Bible stressed the essential equality of man and his humbleness before God. It followed that justice was divine and holy; injustice was a sin. The prophets explained to the temple pilgrims that what counted was not the sacrifice or ritual but the way they behaved toward their fellows. This strong sense of social justice and responsibility was to give rise in later centuries to the idealistic philosophies of social democracy and Zionism. One's purpose and mission as understood by the Jewish mind was to live one's earthly life as a moral being, not because of any reward or retribution nor from fear of punishment; neither because of the prospect of a better life in heaven nor out of a sense of guilt due to some original sin; man was to be good because God is good, and man is created in the image of God.

The written Law of the Torah, evolving out of and including the Ten Commandments, was later amplified in Roman times in the books of the Mishnah and Talmud, and in many subsequent books devoted to Jewish jurisprudence, all sanctified as the word of an abstract deity, God the Lawgiver, as interpreted and implemented by successive generations of wise men, the Rabbis.

As will be noted in a later chapter, the essential dilemma of Israeli politics today arises from the fundamental question: which law is supreme, that drafted by lawyers and parliamentarians in a modern democratic context or that which has been nurtured by generations of pious Jews and has in return sustained them?

History did not let the Jews develop their ethics and jurisprudence in peace, largely because their land lies at the crossroads of Africa, Asia, and Europe, lending it great strategic importance throughout history.

Under pressure from the Dorian-invasion of the Greek mainland, tribes known as the Sea Peoples, including the Philistines (Hebrew pelishtim), migrated from the Aegean isles and invaded the Land of Israel. This onslaught was a major factor in establishing the kingship of Saul in response to the acute need for national unity. The Philistines have long since disappeared from history, leaving little but their name, in the modern English form of "Palestine" derived from the Latin Palaestina. (The Arabic-speaking people who are today known as Palestinians are a mixture of Arabs, Crusaders, Turks, and Egyptians, together with the descendants of some biblical Jews who converted twice, first to Byzantine Christianity, then to Islam. Many Palestinian Arab village names still indicate this Hebrew origin.)

Following the death of Solomon, Jeroboam of the tribe of Ephraim rebelled as the head of a coalition of northern tribes against Solomon's son and successor, Rehoboam, who led only the southern tribes of Judah, Simeon, and Benjamin. The ensuing division between the northern kingdom of Israel and the southern kingdom of Judah served to give a monarchical form to tribal-geographic entities that had existed before the rise of the united monarchy and had maintained their separate identities as administrative units during Solomon's reign. The civil war that broke out between north and south encouraged Shishak, King of Egypt, to invade and plunder Jerusalem.

The two Jewish kingdoms, lasting for several hundred years, intermittently fought off outside enemies. But in 721 BCE, Israel was conquered by the Assyrians (inhabiting present-day Iraq), while the Babylonians, who overthrew the Assyrians, took Jerusalem in 586 BCE. The Temple of Solomon was destroyed, and the Judeans followed their northern brethren into exile.

A reverse in Middle Eastern politics came with the rise of the Persians under Cyrus, who defeated Babylon and permitted the Jews to return from exile to rebuild their Temple in Jerusalem in 538 BCE. Under Ezra and Nehemiah, a small principality, ruled by a Persian "High Commissioner," was established around Jerusalem.

Defeating the Persians, Alexander the Great conquered Jerusalem in 333 BCE. This inaugurated a period of Greek and Hellenistic rule that lasted until 168 BCE, when the Maccabee brothers of Modiin village near Jerusalem led a successful revolt of Jewish peasants that reestablished

Jewish independence. However, the small independent state soon was faced with the might of the Roman Empire. In 63 BCE the Jews were compelled to accept the status of a vassal or client state of Rome. Roman oppression grew in such severity that a major rebellion broke out in 66. Reinforcements were brought by the Romans under Vespasian and Titus, who, after a long and bitter siege, entered Jerusalem and destroyed the Second Temple in the year 70. Razed to the ground, the city was renamed Aelia Capitolina, and no Jew was allowed to live there. The capital even earlier had been moved deliberately to a new Roman city built north of modern Tel Aviv and known as Caesarea. Some ruins of the Second Temple, including the famous Western Wall, may be seen today in Jerusalem.

A small group of Jewish rebels held out at the fortress of Masada near the Dead Sea until 73, when they committed suicide rather than surrender. Roman rule was reimposed with extreme severity, the common punishment for rebels being crucifixion.

Nevertheless, the Jewish leader Bar Kochba headed an uprising in northern Israel for three years, between 132 and 135, followed by another Jewish attempt to throw off Roman rule in 352. When the Persians invaded in 614, in the course of their wars against the Byzantine Romans, they were welcomed by the Jews who remembered the days of Cyrus. But Jewish independence was not yet to be renewed.

The Arabs invaded the ancient Jewish homeland in 636, followed in 1072 by the Seljuk Turks. These were displaced in 1099 by the European Crusaders, who massacred all the Jews they found in Jerusalem. However, under the spiritual leadership of Nachmanides (fl.c. 1267) the Jewish community of Jerusalem was revived and has continued to the present without further interruption. In 1291 the Crusaders were evicted by the Mamluks. In 1517 the Ottoman Turks established the Sanjaq of Jerusalem as an obscure province of their empire. In 1799 Napoleon Bonaparte invaded the Middle East, bringing the revolutionary ideas of liberty, equality, and fraternity. The time had come for the Jews to rise from their ashes like the legendary phoenix.

Political Parties in Israel

THE EARLY HISTORY OF ZIONISM

With only a few minor exceptions, all Israeli parties define themselves as Zionist. When a modern name was sought for the Jewish national liberation movement, "Zionism," or a belief in the organized return to Zion, was adopted at the end of the 19th century. The name "Zion," from the Hebrew word for a dry, rocky hill, referred historically to one of the ridges upon which Jerusalem was built.

The Zionist movement, which today is about 100 years old, has culminated in the reestablishment of Jewish sovereignty in the ancient homeland. Its motivating forces were a desire to reassert Jewish dignity, establish social justice in a Jewish society, escape the anti-Semitic troubles of a non-Jewish environment, and provide an outlet for the creative energy and vitality of the Jews--as Jews.

Following the Roman conquest, enslaved Jews had been sent to all parts of the Roman Empire in Europe and Africa, from where they gradually drifted to almost every country in the world, in large or small groups. Wherever they came, they were invariably treated as outsiders, alien in tongue, fashion, faith, habits, and food customs. They reacted by preserving their insularity, by ignoring the gentile environment as far as possible. The Jews in exile saw their status as temporary, their duty to wait for a divine sign to return home. Never forgetting for a moment the ancient glory of liberty and independence, they prayed daily for the return to Jerusalem.

The opportunity for a new bid for emancipation came with the French Revolution, which tore down the fabric of European empires. As the great Austro-Hungarian and Ottoman conglomerations crumbled and each European people sought and eventually obtained its freedom, the Jews, who had been living among them as yet another minority community, were compelled to rethink their destiny. At first, many Jews in many countries joined the local nationalist movements, either in the honest belief that this was the patriotic thing to do or in order to obtain better conditions for the Jewish minority under whatever new regime would arise. However, it appears that at some stage in their development, European nationalist movements made it clear, with greater or lesser subtlety, to their Jewish supporters that they were not wanted. As European nationalisms grew, the differences between them were sought and exaggerated in an effort to back claims for a territorial basis for new nations, which exercised the minds of politicians, generals, poets, and philosophers, leading ultimately (among other causes) to the two World Wars. The Jews were left in a problematic position: as a self-consciously ex-Asian group with declared spiritual attachments to a territory in the Middle East, they could not logically seek a European destiny. Although some individuals in the Jewish community did argue in favor of assimilation into the Christian nations of Europe, they carried little weight. Intermarriage was no solution, certainly not for the community as a whole.

In 1892 Leo Pinsker published a book called <u>Autoemancipation</u> in the German language in Berlin. This was to become one of the major writings of Zionism. It had been preceded in 1862 by Moses Hess' <u>Rome and Jerusalem</u>, and was followed in 1896 by Theodor Herzl's <u>Judenstaat</u>. These publications represent three stages in the development of the Jewish national movement. Hess was the first to expound the theory that the Jews should go home to rebuild their land. Pinsker elaborated on the need for territorial independence, and his book led to the convening of the <u>Hovevei Zion</u> (Lovers of Zion) movement at a conference in Kattowitz, Russia, in 1894. In 1897 Herzl convened the first Zionist Congress, which formulated the Basle program for the establishment for the Jewish people of a home in Palestine, secured by public law. It is significant that Pinsker, like Hess and Herzl, arrived at a "national" solution of the Jewish Question while living in an "assimilated" environment. Pinsker had been associated with the efforts at "Russification" of the Jews, which were carried on by The Society for the Spread of Culture Among Russian Jews, of which he was one of the founders. He gradually, however, revised his Jewish views, endeavoring after a while to persuade Jewish leaders that the Jewish Question could be settled only by the creation of a Jewish territorial center. It was the anti-Jewish policy of the Russian Czarist government that led Pinsker to emerge as a Jewish nationalist. It was largely at his instance that there was established in Russia The Society for the Support of Jewish Agriculturists and Handicraftsmen in Palestine (Odessa, 1884).[1]

The "political Zionists" who joined Herzl at Basle in 1897 were, however, driven not by religious or philanthropic motives but by a dream of social justice in a land where Jews would have not only freedom from oppression but also full opportunity for expression and achievement. Political Zionism appealed especially to Russian Jews, who were kindled by the revolutionary ferment going on around them. The first Zionist Congress recreated the concept of a Hebrew polity. It turned a spiritual nation into a political nation.

> The Jewish Question was no longer a private matter of Jews; it had become an international question of great political importance. After 1800 years of political inactivity, the Jewish people had returned to play a role in world history.[2]

Zionist activity was not limited to conferences, tracts, and declarations. Small groups of Jews left Europe for Palestine to establish farming villages. The first one was founded in 1878 at Petach Tiqva (a symbolic name meaning gateway to hope) in a swampy region northeast of Jaffa. In the next decade, a string of new villages built by immigrants was established at Rishon Lezion (The First to Zion), Ness Ziona (The Flag of Zion), Rosh Pina (Foundation Stone), and Zichron Yaakov (Memorial to Jacob), on land bought from the Turkish or Arab landowners. Exponents of this direct, agricultural Zionism were such men as Menahem Ussishkin and Nahum Sokolow, supported by the ideologist Ahad Ha'am. Another school of thought, known as political Zionism, led by Herzl and later by Chaim Weizmann, held that internationally accepted arrangements and guarantees were more important than a policy of fait accompli. In retrospect, both were probably right. To facilitate Jewish settlement, which involved purchasing land and equipment, the Jewish Colonial Trust was set up in 1898, followed in 1901 by the Jewish National Fund. In 1908, the Palestine office of the Zionist Organisation was opened, laying the foundation of the future government of Israel. A year later, in 1909, the city of Tel Aviv was founded, followed in 1911 by Degania, Israel's first kibbutz.

The revival of the soil was accompanied by a revival of the Hebrew language. Long confined to ritual purposes, like Latin and Sanskrit, it returned to vernacular use and was the living vehicle of the Jewish renaissance. World War I created the currents of change that were to lead to Jewish independence. The Balfour Declaration of November 2, 1917 and the Bolshevik Revolution of the same year had profound effects on Jewish destiny. The Jewish community of Palestine was placed under strict Turkish surveillance, but this did not prevent some young Jews from organizing the "Nili" spy ring, which helped General Edmund Allenby in his advance on Jerusalem, probably to a greater extent than the much-publicized Bedouin raids on the Turks organized by the British army under Thomas Edward Lawrence. At the San Remo Conference of April 1920, the Mandate for Palestine was assigned to Britain to be administered according to the terms of the Balfour Declaration. After the British-Turkish Peace Treaty was signed at Lausanne in 1922, this arrangement was formally confirmed by the Council of the League of Nations, and provisions were made for the establishment of a Jewish Agency in Palestine, eventually founded in 1929.

THE IDEOLOGICAL GROWTH OF ZIONISM

As noted, Zionism is a central feature of almost all Israeli political parties and movements and is generally accepted as a synonym for Israeli nationalism. The simple identification, however, of Israeli nationhood with Jewish nationhood leads logically to the call for the concentration of all the Jews in the State of Israel, a physical impossibility. But while Zionism insists that only through actually living in Israel as an Israeli citizen can a Jew realize his "Jewishness," the realities of life have compelled a less stark demand, although without abandoning in the slightest the centrality of Israel in Jewish life. Only a small faction, calling themselves the "Canaanites" (a group that was created on May 15, 1948 and has never seriously contested Israeli politics), claim the existence of an Israeli nationality that is divorced from Zionism or Judaism. Another attitude, held by many Jews outside Israel, recognizes the right of a person in a free society to several loyalties, including one's legal obligations in the land of birth and/or residence, as well as an essentially emotional and spiritual commitment toward that small territory, the only one in the world, that is under Jewish sovereignty.

At this point, some statistics must be mentioned: by the almost total destruction of the Jews of Europe by the Nazis during World War II, the number of Jews in the world dropped from 16.7 to 11.0 million and rose to only 14.3 million by 1973. East European Jewry no longer existed, and the center of gravity of the Jewish people was transferred to Western Europe, the British Commonwealth, the United States, and South America. Communist rule cut off 3 million Jews in Russia, denying them participation in Zionist and even Jewish religious activities. In Israel, immigration, largely from the Moslem countries, brought 20 percent of the Jewish people inside the new republic (today, 3 million). In its organizational and ideological values, modern Israel is lineal heir to Eastern and Central European Jewries. Following the Bolshevik Revolution, ties with Russia were cut. But the Russian pioneers who reached Israel before that revolution were to influence strongly the character of the new state.

Faced with disasters of unprecedented magnitude, Zionism in the 1940s took on a revolutionary and militant cast in fighting for independence and in undertaking simultaneous tasks of land reclamation, refugee settlement, cultural rehabilitation, military growth, and the establishment of the organs of state. The catalyst of Arab objections to Zionism has been of immense value in strengthening and building Israel; the oft-proclaimed threat of being thrown into the sea only has made the Israelis even more self-reliant. Meanwhile, the debate continues: how to relate ancient values and traditions to modernity.

The background must be reexamined for an understanding of the ideological problem: The Jews largely had failed in the conscious bid made by some of their number, in the 19th century, to become like the European Christians. European anti-Semitism fed on ancient Christian prejudices against a people that had refused to accept Jesus Christ and had allegedly "killed the Christian God." Orthodox Judaism had to contend with universalistic, rationalistic, liberal, and also socialist ideas. The Zionist solution sought to resolve these dilemmas in a political fashion and in a familiar territorial context. Zionism did not seek territorial unification, as in Germany or Italy, but the territorial concentration in the original motherland of a long-scattered nation. It is interesting to note that "the enemy," a factor appearing in the mythology of so many other nationalisms, was almost absent from Zionism. The conflict with Britain never was regarded as the supreme expression of Zionism. European anti-Semitism was fought wherever possible, but the main effort was aimed at removing the Jews of Europe out of harm's way. The clash with the Arabs, while it may have unfortunately assumed quite apocalyptic dimensions for some Arab thinkers and leaders, has not been so seen on the Israeli side, where the conflict is regarded as tragic and unnecessary.

The point of departure for Zionism was that all Jews outside Israel lived as an alien minority, whether they were aware of the fact or not. Only in Israel could the Jew live as part of a dominant, majority culture without looking over his shoulder to see what people would say about him. Minority life invited indignities. After some hesitation, due to a variety of reasons, most Jews around the world are indicating their acceptance of this logic. Not surprisingly, in some democratic countries where legal and physical conditions for Jewish minority survival are easier, Zionist logic is somewhat less persuasive and Jews are able to accept and rationalize their minority status; but the defiantly Zionist revival of Jewish youth born and bred in conditions of strict Communist control has proved recently that Soviet ideology is unable to change the character of an ancient people. As Leo Pinsker pointed out decades ago, even legal rights did not change popular prejudices:

> Among the living, the Jew was considered dead;
> among the citizens, an alien; among the settled
> population, a wanderer and a sojourner; in the
> eyes of patriots, a stranger without a country
> of his own, and in the eyes of all of them, a
> hated rival.

Herzl's theories resemble those of Pinsker, regarding the establishment of a Jewish state as the only solution. Herzl noted that the definition of an alien was always made by the dominant majority and was essentially a question of power. Max Nordau (1849-1923) felt that a state of national emergency existed for the Jewish people and that action should be sweeping and immediate. The future of Jewish culture was the concern of Asher Ginsburg (1856-1924), better known as Ahad Ha'am. He felt that only by developing the Hebrew language and the Jewish culture of Palestine would a nucleus be created to hold the Jewish people together. In broadening the concept of Jewish culture beyond strict religious tradition, Ahad Ha'am established the patterns of modern Israeli education. J. H. Brenner (1880-1920) thought that the years of exile had created a negative

Jewish character, which could only be removed through creative labor in conditions of freedom. The Jewish individual,
emancipating himself from the deadening bonds of tradition,
seeks to maintain and develop his Jewish character in his
natural surroundings. Hence, Brenner's negation of cosmo-
politan revolutionism. Martin Buber (1878-1965) sought a
new interpretation for the spiritual values of Judaism.
The Jew inherits an ancient tradition, yet is faced by
alien cultural pressures. The contradiction can be resolved
only by affirmation of the internal essence. This is the
personal redemption of the Jew. The public interpretation
of this redemption can be brought to fruition only in freedom, in a national Jewish state. Buber felt that Judaism
aspires to union with God and the world but calls for action here and now, placing a higher value on deeds than on
consciousness or experience--religiously speaking. Deed
and not faith is the decisive bond between man and God.
The future in Judaism, wrote Buber, is an earthly future,
for human liberation through deliberate effort. Socialism
was an imperfect and partial creation of this attitude.
After Israel's independence, Buber maintained that the state
would justify itself only if it served as an instrument for
the realization of Jewish destiny. His views were upheld
and amplified by David Ben Gurion, who stressed Israel's
duty to itself to be a nation of the highest moral caliber.
In A. D. Gordon (1857-1922) Jewish nationalism with a
strong socialist slant was raised almost to the rank of a
new religion. In poetic and often mystical language, Gordon spoke of the "marriage" of the Jew to the soil of his
homeland, sanctified through labor. His teachings led to
the growth of a nonclass-conscious socialism among early
Jewish pioneers.

Jewish socialism fought against discrimination in work
against Jews and saw in these efforts a way of rehabilitating the anomalous economic structure of the Jewish people.
On an existential plane, the Jewish socialists saw labor as
the rejuvenator of the individual and the community. The
intellectual tradition of the Israeli left wing flowed
naturally from thinkers who underlined the nonspiritual,
economic nature of Jewish nationhood. And they did so,
paradoxically, with true religious fervor.

Ber Borochov, who died in 1918 at the age of 36, was
the founder of Zionist Marxism. Adding the term "conditions
of production" to Marxist "relations of production," Borochov argued that these preconditions include territory and
resources, neither of which the Jews had in the absence of

independence. Only in a free Jewish state could a proper Jewish class war take place, and Jewish socialism become a possibility. Indeed, the Jewish labor movement in Israel was not principally the result of objective local economic conditions but rather of an imported idea, quite foreign to the Ottoman Empire and its sleepy province of Palestine. Nachman Syrkin, continuing this approach, saw the free Jew as the true socialist revolutionary, rising from tragedy to a lofty historic mission, bringing justice to the oppressed of the world. The strong idealism of Borochov and Syrkin led to the establishment of collective (kibbutz) and communal (moshav) villages by Jewish pioneers. Nonreligious socialist Zionism was paralleled by a traditional Zionism drawing directly from religious roots.

Traditional religious Judaism has not yet resolved the problems of its relationships with the modern State of Israel. The problems have been both fundamental and practical. Fundamentally speaking, Judaism recognizes no other lawgiver but God. How then could legislation by a parliament of mortals be regarded? To what extent could a religious Jew accept secular legislation in a declaredly Jewish state? What would be the position of the hierarchy of the Israeli Rabbinate in the state? How could the machinery and vital services of a nation stop for 24 hours on the Sabbath (Saturday), on which the Bible forbids the Jew to work? These problems and many others have been solved in patchwork fashion by compromise arrangements within the context of Israeli coalition politics, but they will continue to be live election issues in the future. Abraham Isaac Kook, for 14 years Chief Rabbi of Mandatory Palestine, evolved a religious national theory that attempted to overcome these problems. He saw the people of Israel, as taught in the Bible, to be a "holy nation," and Jewish history to be the "ideal essence" of human history. Israel, the people, had retreated from holiness while in exile and could only return to holiness through its national redemption and freedom. If Israel is capable of walking in the light of divine grace, the whole world will emulate her. Rabbi Kook negated the condition of exile, which did not permit true Jewish existence, for only in the Holy Land could a Holy People be true to itself. Immigrants, even those not avowedly religious, such as the socialist and Marxist elements, were considered by Kook to be performing a religious act of great merit, by their very immigration.

Religious Jews nevertheless ponder deeply whether the secularization of modern Israel is a departure from the will of God or whether the establishment and victories of the young state are signs of God's blessing. The present status quo has been criticized strongly by such intellectuals as Isaiah Leibowitz, arguing that Israel's independence was a purely secular and political act, devoid of any religious significance; that religion and state must be separated and religion divorced from politics. It appears that there is growing support for his ideas, largely among the Israeli youth.

Another major trend in Zionism has been strongly nationalistic. Ze'ev Jabotinsky (1880-1940), who saw himself as the successor to Herzl and Nordau, stood in opposition to the cautious Weizmann and founded the Revisionist Zionist movement. He called for an open declaration by Zionism that it stood for a Jewish state on both banks of the River Jordan and insisted on mass immigration leading to early independence. Jabotinsky stressed the pride of Israel's past:

> Each and every one of us has behind him or her seventy generations of literate ancestors, who learned and spoke about God and history, about the ideas of justice, about the problems of humanity and the future. In this sense every Jew is a prince.

This vision Jabotinsky sought to realize through a belligerent and young Jewry liberating the people, chivalrous, noble, and aristocratic.

Jabotinsky rejected socialism, saying that it would distract from devotion to Zionism. His followers--who took up arms against the British, at times in open defiance of the socialist leadership of the Jews in Palestine--today form the Herut party. (These followers are part of the Likud Union.)

To sum up, both Jewish and Israeli nationalities today stand on a series of attachments and attitudes rather than a distinct pattern of theory. Several cases that come before the Supreme Court of Israel have raised the legal question of "who is a Jew," with learned judges giving conflicting opinions.

> Even if we do not accept Jewish faith or Jewish culture as an objective entity compelling itself upon every Jew, there is in the individual Jew a definite pattern of urges and tendencies, priorities and desires. The moment the Jew recognises that he is different and seeks to define this difference, one can say that the relation between

himself and Jewish existence in the sovereign
State of Israel is quantitative rather than qualitative. Zionism's special character lies in defining that Jewish existence in Israel is the
most authentic Jewish existence. It is the most
authentic not because it imposes Jewish content
but on the contrary because it leaves unlimited
room for experiment and encounter with the world,
which does not lead beyond the Jewish fold. In
a world that is becoming more and more uniform,
the Jew seeks to play his distinct role. Instead of mass culture and universal means of communication, blurring ethnic and cultural identities, the Jew seeks to retain his own culture,
and Israel is his instrument.[3]

NOTES

1. P. Goodman, "Foreword" to L. Pinsker, Autoemancipa-
tion (Eng. lang. ed.; New York: Massada, 1939), p. 1.
2. J. Klausner, "Foreword" to The Protocols of the
First Zionist Congress in Basle, 1897 (Hebrew ed.; Jerusalem: Jewish Agency, 1946).
3. I. Kolatt, Theories of Israeli Nationalism (Jerusalem: World Zionist Organisation, 1969). See also A.
Arian, Consensus in Israel (New York: General Learning
Press Reprint, 1971).

2

THE EMBRYO STATE: ITS INSTITUTIONS AND PARTIES

THE ELECTED ASSEMBLIES

The Mandatory period, which lasted for the 30 years from 1918 to 1948, has become known colloquially in Israel as the period of "the embryo state," hamedinah shebaderech, or literally, "the state on the way." Indeed, although Israel formally declared her independence in 1948, that declaration would have remained on paper without the solid and steady growth of the Jewish community and its institutions under, and often despite, foreign rule.

The Mandate of the League of Nations, Article 3 states: "The Mandatory shall, so far as circumstances permit, encourage local autonomy."

The British authorities had inherited the millet (community) system of the Ottoman Empire, under which each community, defined religiously, was allowed a degree of internal autonomy. In a far-flung empire, the principle of divide and rule satisfied both the Sultan and his subjects. The British accordingly allowed the Jewish community in Palestine to continue running its own administration but also actively encouraged the growth of a parallel Arab Palestinian administration, in order to play off one side against the other.[1]

Article 83 of the Palestine Order-in-Council, 1922,[2] provided inter alia that every religious community established and exercising jurisdiction at the time of the order was to enjoy autonomy for the internal affairs of the community subject to the provisions of any ordinance or order issued by the High Commissioner. Soon after the advent of the (British) Civil Administration in June 1920, the Jewish community, of its own initiative, organized elections on a voluntary basis for the purposes of electing a lay body to represent its interests before government. Local committees also were elected in towns and settlements. These organs functioned fairly satisfactorily and served with a measure of success the purpose for which they were created, but had no official sanction or constitutional basis. Government was therefore pressed to provide statutory form and authority for them, and in due course did so by means of a set of regulations made in 1927 under an enabling law known as the Religious Communities (Organisation) Ordinance, 1926. This ordinance was derived from and designed to implement Article 83 of the Palestine Order-in-Council, 1922, cited above. The 1925 ordinance, being of a general character, was to serve also, if necessary, for the recognition and self-regulation of other religious communities in Palestine and was so intended, but in fact no other community applied to government to be recognized under the ordinance.[3] The Jewish community rules, 1927, in substance gave statutory effect to the voluntary lay and religious organs of the Jewish community already described. The lay organs of the community were (1) an Elected Assembly (Asefat Hanivharim), (2) a General Council (Vaad Leumi), and (3) committees of local communities. The election rules of 1930 defined the constitution and systems of elections to the Elected Assembly. These elections were general, direct, equal, secret, and proportional. Every Jew of either sex whose name was included in the Register of the Jewish community (known as Knesset Yisrael) and who had attained the age of 20 years was entitled to vote. Every Jew whose name was included in the Register of the community, who had attained the age of 25 years, had been resident in Palestine not less than one year, and could read and write Hebrew was eligible to be elected as a member of the Elected Assembly.

The Elected Assembly comprised 71 persons originally, equivalent to the number of members of the Sanhedrin, which was the supreme court at the time of the Second Temple. The Elected Assembly in turn elected a smaller number constituting the Vaad Leumi, which again, in turn, for administrative reasons, appointed from among its members a small executive committee (Vaad Poel). The functions of the Vaad Leumi comprised the administration of the lay affairs of the community.

On October 25, 1920, the first Elected Assembly met in Jerusalem. A total of four assemblies were elected by the community, the number of seats contested varying from one election to the next.

In the first Elected Assembly, about one-third of all seats were won by Zionist socialist groups, about a half by the urban business community of largely Sephardi Jews (descendants of Jews evicted from Spain in 1492) of Jerusalem, Jaffa, and Tiberias, and less than a fifth by religious groups, largely from Jerusalem, Hebron, and Safed. Other small factions such as the Yemenite immigrants, the Farmers' Association (private landowners), the Progressives (a liberal group), and the Clerks' Union also won seats.

Elections to the first Elected Assembly were rocked by controversy. The subject was female suffrage, to which the orthodox elements of the community objected. At the elections, special polls were set up for the Orthodox Jews who had excluded their women from voting, and each vote was in effect given double weight. When the assembly refused to eliminate the clause in the election regulations granting women full suffrage, the orthodox members withdrew from it. This withdrawal eventually was to facilitate the development of Israel in the direction of secular democracy.

In the second Elected Assembly, 1925, 29 parties contested the elections. The labor parties won a total of 38 percent of the seats; the Sephardis, only 9 percent; the Revisionist Zionists, 7 percent; and the other parties barely managed to get a seat each. Although not attaining an absolute majority, the predominant position of labor in Israel was already clear. The 1931 elections confirmed labor leadership under the evolving Mapai party. The third Elected Assembly remained in office for 13 years, although legally its term should have expired after three years. The long deferment of elections, due initially to difficulties with the voters' register, was largely the result of fateful events that absorbed all of the community's energies. Because of the Arab riots of 1936-39, the ensuing political uncertainty, and the outbreak of World War II, the fourth Elected Assembly was not elected until 1944.

In the fourth Elected Assembly, 171 seats were contested by 12 parties. The Revisionist and religious parties boycotted the elections owing to disputes with labor leaders, thus conceding a clear labor victory. It appeared that nonlabor Zionists preferred to consolidate their positions in local government and did not then compete effectively with labor for national dominance.[4]

The groups that submitted lists for elections to the assemblies fell into a number of categories. First in size and importance were the Zionist parties consisting of the three major camps: labor, religious, and nationalist (Re-

TABLE 1

Composition of the Four Elected Assemblies

	Seats	Percent-age	Turnout (%)
The First Elected Assembly (April 19, 1920)			77
Labour			
Ahdut Ha'avoda	70	22.3	
Hapoel Hatsair	41	13.1	
Communists	--	--	
Yemenites	12	3.8	
Sephardi	60	19.1	
Religious	64	20.4	
Revisionist	--	--	
Various middle-class lists	67	21.3	
Women's Rights League	--	--	
The Second Elected Assembly (December 6, 1925)			56.7
Labour			
Ahdut Ha'avoda	54	24.4	
Hapoel Hatsair	30	13.6	
Communists	6	2.7	
Yemenites	20	9.0	
Sephardi	20	9.0	
Religious	19	8.6	
Middle-class lists	44	19.9	
Women's Rights League	13	5.0	
The Third Elected Assembly (January 15, 1931)			56.2
Labour			
Mapai	31	43.7	
Poalei Zion	1	1.4	
Communists	2	2.8	
Yemenites	3	4.2	
Religious	5	7.0	
Revisionists	15	21.1	
Middle-class lists	14	19.7	
The Fourth Elected Assembly (August 1944)			67
Mapai	63	52.9	
Mapam	21	17.6	
Religious	17	14.3	
New Immigrants (Progressive)	18	15.1	

Source: A. Etzioni, Alternative Ways to Democracy--
The Example of Israel (Jerusalem: Hebrew University,
1966).

visionist). Within each of these camps there were divisions that rested often on doctrinal niceties and produced a succession of party splits, mergers, and changes of framework that have continued to this day. Nevertheless, the several mainstream Zionist parties largely preserved their identities and have remained to dominate Israel's political landscape. A different category of parties was that based upon communal, occupational, or local interests. None of these has ever been very successful.

The coalition cabinets that have always governed Israel are a legacy of the prestate community as much as the country's major parties. In the community that was a voluntary organization from a legal point of view, broad coalitions were both necessary and advisable. Therefore, the National Council was always representative of all but the tiniest factions in the Elected Assembly. The small cabinetlike Executive Council (Vaad Poel) was only slightly less representative of the varied political opinions in the community. The Elected Assembly had to meet at least once a year to perform three statutory duties: to vote a budget, set tax rates, and elect a new National Council. The budget debate enabled Assemblymen to express their views on all questions of community importance. The Elected Assembly did not attract the interest it merited as a parliamentary platform for a number of reasons. Although it was the central forum of the community, it met at most for a few days each year while it left the surveillance of community affairs to the Executive Council. Other organizations operating in the Jewish community, such as the General Federation of Labour (Histadrut), the Jewish Agency (Sochnut Yehudit), and local village and town councils, tended to be parallel foci of power. The community was still very much a junior partner in its alliance with the World Zionist Organisation. The Zionist Congress, which met at intervals in and outside Palestine, was thought of as the parliament of the "state in embryo" rather than the Elected Assembly, which represented the Jews of Palestine.

However, history was to link the Elected Assembly with the Knesset of independent Israel by strong ties: out of the 171 members of the Fourth Elected Assembly, at least 55 were later elected to the Knesset. In 1971 there were 10 assembly veterans in the Knesset. The close connection between the Elected Assembly and the Knesset was capped in the person of Joseph Sprinzak, who, after serving as a member of the Presidium of the assembly from its inception with but few interruptions, was elected the First Knesset Speaker, in which capacity he served for over 10 years until his death in 1959.

Symbolically, the fourth Elected Assembly dissolved itself on February 13, 1949, on the eve of the convocation of the Constituent Assembly of the State of Israel. However, this central community organization virtually had ceased to function nine months earlier, with the Declaration of Independence.

At the end of the Mandate, Britain did not take any steps to ensure the smooth transfer of power to the Jewish state that was to come into being by virtue of the UN resolution of November 29, 1947. The liquidation of the British administration was carried out under conditions calculated to produce maximum chaos and to improve the Arab military position.[5]

The Trans-Jordanian Arab Legion led by the British officer Glubb Pasha attacked Jewish Jerusalem in 1947-48, while British army camps and police forts throughout Palestine were handed over to local Arab irregulars. Jewish paramilitary forces often were disarmed forcibly by British troops, and several Jewish guerrillas were hanged.

As the Mandate ended, the armies of Egypt, Jordan, Iraq, Syria, and Lebanon readied for an assault on the infant Jewish state, the first of a long series of acts of aggression.

INDEPENDENCE: THE INTERIM PERIOD

As the end of the British Mandate drew near, the steering committee of the Zionist Organisation met on April 12, 1948 in Tel Aviv to establish interim arrangements. A People's Council (Moetset Ha'am) of 37 members was set up, led by a smaller People's Administration (Minhelet Ha'am) of 13 members.

The People's Council met on May 14, 1948, the day the British left the country, at a historic meeting in Tel Aviv in which David Ben Gurion read out Israel's Declaration of Independence. Israel was promptly recognized by the United States and the Soviet Union, and invaded by the Arabs.

The People's Administration became the Provisional Government of the State of Israel, while the People's Council, renamed the Council of State, was later to evolve into the Knesset. The suggestion to have a parliament of 120 members was made by Z. Warhaftig of the religious parties, reviving the tradition of the Great Assembly of the Jewish people (Knesset Gedolah) in the days of Persian administration, in which, according to the Talmud, there were 120 members.[6]

TABLE 2

Composition of the People's Council

Party	Number of Members
Labour	
Mapai	10
Mapam	5
Religious	
Mizrahi ⎫	
Hapoel ⎬	5
Hamizrahi ⎭	
Agudat Yisrael	3
Nationalist	
Revisionist ⎫	
Zionists ⎬	3
General Zionist	6
Wizo	1
New Immigrants	1
Yemenites	1
Sephardi	1
Communist	1
Total	37

TABLE 3

Composition of the People's Administration

Party	Number of Members
Labour	
Mapai	4
Mapam	2
Religious	
Mizrahi ⎫	
Hapoel-Hamizrahi ⎬	3
Agudat Yisrael ⎭	
Nationalist	
General Zionist ⎫	
Sephardi ⎬	4
New Immigrants ⎭	
Total	13

The number of members had indeed fluctuated widely: from 314 in the first Elected Assembly to 221 in the second and third, reduced to 171 in the fourth, then to an emergency minimum of 37 in the People's Council. Bearing in mind Israel's small population, the tendency was to have a smaller legislature.

During the Mandatory period, prototype political institutions of Israel were formed that laid the basis for much of her later political life. The masses and elites gained experience, well before independence, in the functioning of democratic political institutions.[7]

The transition from an informal, voluntary community to a republican democracy, bureaucratized and formalized, with normative values and legal instruments, was a profound change. The Jews of Palestine were no longer part of a triple society: Jewish-Arab-British. They were independent and on a new course. Nevertheless, the traditions and experience of 50 years had created sufficient social cohesiveness to meet the new challenges effectively. The pressures of war forced upon the infant republic acted as a powerful catalyst to national unity and overcame to a large degree the ills of "a sorry regime of factions," which David Ben Gurion feared would weaken Israeli democracy.[8]

NOTES

1. M. H. Bernstein, The Politics of Israel, The First Decade of Statehood (Princeton, N.J.: Princeton University Press, 1957), pp. 13-16.

2. The Palestine Royal Commission Memoranda, Colonial No. 133, London, 1937, p. 101.

3. This indicates the degree of disorganization among the Arabs of Palestine--despite British efforts to establish the Mufti Haj Amin al-Husseini as head of the Arab Moslem community. The internal crisis of leadership that persists today among the Arabs of Palestine has been a major factor in the historical and political development of the Middle East and is a prime cause of the Palestine problem. The inability to establish self-rule, as the Jews of Palestine did, and the rejection of Palestinian independence-- by the Palestinians themselves--when offered it in 1947 by the United Nations, stand in sorry contrast to the growth of Israeli democracy. See Report by the High Commissioner for Palestine on the Elections for the Palestine Legislative Council, 1923, Command Paper 1889, London, 1923.

4.   E. Guttman, <u>Israel Government</u> (Hebrew ed.; Jerusalem: Hebrew University Student's Union Press, 1970), p.
61.

5.   Bernstein, op. cit., p. 21.

6.   <u>Babylonian Talmud, Tractate Megilla, 17</u>, quoted
in <u>The Legislature, Debates and Conclusions</u> (Hebrew ed.;
Jerusalem: Constitutional Committee, Provisional Council,
State of Israel, 1949), p. 17.

7.   E. Reich, "Israel," in <u>Governments and Politics of
the Contemporary Middle East</u>, ed. I. Y. Tareq (Alberta,
1970), p. 253.

8.   Knesset Debates, February 14, 1951.

3

POLITICAL DEVELOPMENT
AFTER INDEPENDENCE

> A state is not manufactured by declaration. It
> is set up anew day after day, by toil incessant
> and the labour of years. A people unfit and un-
> ready to sustain the duty of sufficing unto it-
> self will not preserve freedom even after it is
> won.[1]

Surrounded by hostile countries on all sides and having had to fight four wars within 25 years, Israel may be
described as a "garrison democracy." During her first 20
years Israel experienced 15 changes of government, which
could suggest greater instability than in fact prevailed.
Actually, only 50 people filled some 275 incumbencies as
ministers during this period. A multiparty system with
doctrinal parties should have undergone, it would seem, an
experience like that of the Fourth Republic in France,
where the cabinet was subordinate to the legislature and
plagued by immobilisme, or paralysis. In fact, Israel's
government functioned more like that of Britain, in which
the cabinet, far from being a creature of the legislature,
actually dominated it.[2] Israeli coalition governments have
given the country a balanced and fairly stable administration. No other country of the Middle East can claim such
a record of internal stability, with the total absence of
coups d'etat. David Ben Gurion adapted for Israeli use
the principles of cohesive coalition government with the
formation of the first cabinet in 1949. Mapai had won 46
seats out of 120, or 36 percent of the vote. As leader of
the largest party, Ben Gurion laid down these conditions
for participation in the coalition:

1. cabinet decisions by majority vote
2. collective responsibility of all coalition partners
for all coalition decisions

The compromise arrangements negotiated by coalition partners
are presented to the Knesset as the "Basic Principles of
the Government" when the new cabinet seeks a vote of confidence. These precedents have become fixed procedures and
have been defined in law.[3] <u>No Israeli government has ever
fallen due to a vote of no confidence in the Knesset</u>. Cabinets have fallen due to coalition crises, internal party
disputes, or personal friction, but never by decision of
the Knesset. Changes in government policies have invariably taken place due to internal party pressures, intracoali-
tion agreements, or public opinion, but, again, not because
of Knesset action. If anything, the Knesset has tended to
amplify government policy and reinforce it. The Prime Minister is not free to choose his (or her) ministers. Coalition parties will nominate "their" ministers, and even
within the Labour Party the Prime Minister has to take bloc
pressures into account. In Mapai (part of the Labour Party),
the party leadership has generally--but not exclusively--
been synonymous with the Mapai ministers, the Prime Minister being also party leader. (So far, all Israeli Prime
Ministers have come from Mapai.)[4]

Israeli elections are proportional. While the sorry
experience of the Weimar Republic tended to give proportional representation and coalition governments a bad name
among political scientists, the stability of the Israeli
coalitions, elected on the basis of what one observer calls
"perfect proportionality,"[5] has been due perhaps to the
fact that political life in Israel has been dominated more
by the necessity of constructing and defending a state
rather than by the different conceptions of how this state
should be run. Studies of European coalition governments
seem to justify the construction of an index of stability
based on the number of changes in the party composition of
government, particularly changes of the largest party in
the coalition.[6] Reviewing the "unipolar" democracies of
Europe--namely, Norway, Sweden, Denmark, Iceland, Italy,
and France*--in all cases one finds that one party is always easily the largest in the legislature and is always,

---

*Holland, with a nonunipolar, multiparty, proportion-
ally elected parliament, is quite stable.

or nearly always, in office, either alone or with some smaller partners. In a unipolar system, the dominant party normally holds about 40 percent of the votes and seats while no other party can aspire to even 30 percent. In Sweden, for example, the Social Democrats regularly held over 46 percent of the votes, with no other party being able to exceed 25 percent. The parallel with Labour dominance in Israel since the 1930s is obvious. It is indeed remarkable to note how similar the Israeli political spectrum is to that of a typical West European country.

Following the methodological analysis of J. Jupp,[7] Israel may be classified as standing between two group systems: the multiparty system (within which Jupp places Israel) and the dominant party system. This is because whereas in theory Israel indeed fits the description given by Jupp of a country "where no party commands a clear majority and governments are normally composed of coalitions," the history of Israeli politics shows that for the last four decades one party, Mapai (the leader of the labor movement), has been dominant through elections, with other parties allowed to function in supporting, or opposition, roles. Jupp has placed India in this latter category, and indeed the similarities between Mapai and the Congress Party are striking. Both grew out of, and led, a national liber-

TABLE 4

The Political Spectrum

Typical Country of Western Europe	Israel
Communists	Communists
Left socialists	Mapam
Social Democrats	Labour (Mapai)
Liberals	Independent Liberals, Civil Rights Movement
Agrarian parties	Kibbutz, moshav lobbies (affiliated to Labour, Mapam, and so on)
Christian religious groups	Jewish religious groups
Conservatives	Liberal--Herut bloc (Likud)
Protest groups	Haolam Hazeh (New Force, Black Panthers, and so on)
Ethnic minority groups	Arab parties

ation movement against British rule; both stood for social democracy and parliamentary government; and both have been able to steer their nations to independence despite the fanaticism of their neighbors. Both parties have had to modify their early zeal in tacit or open compromise with other political forces in the arena, while retaining all the while a strong position of leadership, reinforced by popular vote.[8]

The outside observer immediately will recognize a striking resemblance between the party panoramas of India and Israel. Indeed, the historical development was similar: ancient independence and glory, producing great works of religion, art, and culture, followed by many centuries of foreign misrule and economic backwardness, culminating in both cases in a liberation struggle against the very same imperial rulers, and suffering in parallel the agonies of partition, war, and grave refugee problems. Both countries were able to weld together disparate elements of the population, despite severe language problems. The (ruling) Congress Party is paralleled by the Israel Labour Party. The Indian Socialist Party is a counterpart of Mapam. Center groups such as Swatantra find a common language with the Israeli Liberal Party, while the strong nationalism of Herut and the Jana Sangh has much in common. One also may see the affinity between such communal groups as the Hindu Mahasabha or Akali Dal and Israel's religious parties in their advocacy of theocratic ideas. Historically, one may see similarities between Jawaharlal Nehru and David Ben Gurion, between Martin Buber and Mahatma Gandhi (as moral leaders), between Shastri and Eshkol, and perhaps between Golda Meir and Indira Gandhi. Ignoring for a moment the vast disparity in size between Israel and India, one may remark upon the determination of both societies to preserve parliamentary democracy in the face of the most trying odds. Indeed, both countries, which reached independence in almost the same year, have known a wealth of common experiences, hopes, successes, and, sometimes, failures. To date this common history has been recognized mainly by the trade unions and cooperative movements of India, who have sent over 150 trainees to courses arranged by the Histadrut through the Afro-Asian Institute for Labour and Cooperation Studies in Tel Aviv.

Israel had political parties before she had a sovereign parliament. These parties grew out of interacting and sometimes rival forces within four often overlapping spheres of political action: the Zionist Organisation, the Jewish Agency, local town and village councils, and the General Federation of Labour. The fifth field of official Jewish

23

political activity, the embryo parliament of the Elected
Assembly, lacked prestige in comparison with the other four.
Jewish political leaders during the Mandatory period often
served in two, three, four, or even all five fields either
at the same time or interchangeably, thus gaining much
practical experience in "nation building." At the same
time, the lack of prestige of the Elected Assembly and the
preference for utilization of nonparliamentary channels of
government under the Mandate eventually was to have a definite bearing on the status and power of the Knesset in its
relationship with other foci of power after independence.
Israeli parties were never confined to a parliamentary role,
as will be explained further on. Following the definition
of "party" given by J. S. Coleman and quoted by Jupp,[9] one
may say that Israeli parties in the Mandatory period were
associations formally--albeit at first informally--organized
with the explicit and declared purpose of acquiring and/or
maintaining legal control, either singly or in coalition or
electoral competition with other similar associations, over
the personnel, the citizens, and the policy of the government, of a prospective sovereign state. As noted, the system presently obtaining in Israel may be defined as standing midway between the multiparty and dominant party systems. Yet, as far as trends of the 1970s may be discerned,
there is a strong probability of Israeli politics shifting
toward what Jupp calls a distinct bipartisan system,[10] in
which the two major blocs in parliament are the more socialist and the less so. Essentially, Jupp notes, a multiparty system should not have permanent alliances, forcing
a two-party confrontation. However, it would appear in Israel that the socialist-led coalitions, under Mapai, increasingly may face a gradually cohering opposition of the
center right and religious parties, which could possibly,
in some future election, be successful enough to form a
nonsocialist government. Jupp specifically mentions the
stability of Israeli coalitions as a unique phenomenon,
resting on a national unity that is made of more durable
stuff than coalition agreements. This national stability
ultimately rests on a cultural, linguistic, religious, historical, emotional, and sociological continuity 4,000 years
old. Political change therefore occurs in Israel within a
fairly broad and relatively stable nationalist context.
Jupp notes that the process of change from a multi- to a
two-party system may arise through electoral change of system, the consolidation of coalitions along radical-conser-
vative lines, or the lessening of tensions among different

segments of society. In Israel, political leaders have on occasion expressed the belief that adoption of the constituency system instead of proportional representation would drastically reduce the number of parties, which at present number about 10, already a large reduction from the over 20 that contested early elections. A major advocate of this reform was former Prime Minister David Ben Gurion; the matter arises perennially in debate but so far no major change has taken place. With the formation of the Israel Labour Alignment and the parallel growth of the Herut-liberal bloc, which has also become a united party (the Likud), it seems that Israeli political groups are indeed coalescing around several major foci.

Israel's population of 3 million includes Jewish immigrants from a hundred lands as well as a large minority (14 percent) of Arabs (Moslems, Christians, and Druzes). The voting patterns of the population, which show remarkable stability, indicate the rapid social and political integration of the immigrant population. This will be discussed in detail further on. The Jewish Agency, which was largely responsible for bringing in and settling these immigrants, is itself governed by a coalition of all major Israeli parties except the Communists. The strongest partner is the Labour Alignment, whose members usually hold such key positions in the Jewish Agency as chairman of the executive board in Jerusalem, heads of departments of settlement and absorption of new immigrants, of education, and youth. The General Federation of Labour (Histadrut), which has its headquarters in Tel Aviv, also is governed by a committee in which the Labour Alignment predominates. Originally founded as a federation of trade unions, it has become the second largest employer in the country (after the government), an economic empire of 215,000 people in 2,000 cooperatives. Various political parties of the left, and latterly of the center-right too, use the Histadrut as a lobby for their activities.

The importance of the Histadrut and Jewish Agency lies in the fact that they are far older than the state of which they are now part, and which they had worked to establish. The "parental" attitude of authority and experience vis-à-vis the newly established state bureaucracy has been an understandable problem of quasi-constitutional dimensions. The Jewish Agency, through the Zionist Organisation, also constitutes the functional link between Israel and Jewish communities throughout the world and is a major channel for the influx of financial donations, loans, and grants from Jews abroad.*

Until very recently, nearly all political activity in Israel was carried out through the veteran "political establishment." It is only lately that new forms of political activity—such as student dissent, press campaigns by intellectual groups, and public polemics and agitation by independent circles—have developed. Whether these will in due course be absorbed and institutionalized remains to be seen. At least in part one may attribute these developments to the broad publicity given in Israel to youthful and intellectual dissent in the United States, and there is little doubt that the relaxing of border tensions between the 1970 cease-fire and the 1973 war enabled the Israeli public to devote more of its concern to internal matters. Indeed, it was only natural that the Israelis should (as soon as security seemed to have been assured) have reverted to radicalism, because (at the risk of broad generalization) one may say

---

*There are Zionist organizations in all nonsocialist countries. In some countries there are Zionist federations in which all the Zionist parties and organizations are affiliated. The parties and organizations affiliated to the World Zionist Organisation are listed below, together with their representation at the 26th Zionist Congress, convened in Jerusalem (December 20, 1964–January 10, 1965).

Ichud Olami Poaled Zion (World Union of Labour Zionists), connected to Israel's Labour Party (Mapai)—154 seats,

The World Union of General Zionists, connected to Israel's Likud Party—95 seats,

The World Confederation of General Zionists, not connected to any Israeli party—81 seats,

Mizrahi-Hapoel Hamizrahi, connected to Israel's National Religious Party—69 seats,

Herut-Hatsohar (Revisionists), connected to Israel's Herut Party—53 seats,

The World Union of Mapam, connected to Israel's Mapam Socialist Party—35 seats,

The World Union of Ahdut-Ha'avoda-Poalei-Zion, connected to Israel's Ahdut Ha'avoda Party—27 seats.

The Women's International Zionist Organisation (Wizo), connected to Wizo in Israel (no longer a political party but a welfare movement)—12 seats,

Independent Zionist Movement, connected to the Independent Liberal Party in Israel—2 seats.

that Jews, in their political outlook, wherever they may live, have invariably tried to be optimistic, progressive, and forward-looking. The Jew strives for a better world and is often found in the thick and at the front of movements for social reform. Even the very Jewish radical outside Israel, who may ignore, or deny, his Jewishness, is the product of its messianic fervor.[11] This outlook, a product of the Jewish value system, constitutes a political style, an approach to the issues of social organization. Implicit in this style is the view that man and his environment are malleable, that he is much more the creator of his history than its product. Implicit too is the notion that man's environment and his polity are made for him. Implicit is a dynamic view of law, that it is changing and made for man; and especially implicit in such a style is the belief that what happens in this life on this earth is very important.[12] Jewish immigrants to America, like those who went to Israel, brought with them a strong socialist fervor; and, with the decline of American socialism, they became liberals and democrats, often supporting pacifist or non-Jewish liberal causes--such as civil rights for the blacks and Chicanos.[13]

Yet, despite the variety of ideological approaches within Zionism, most Israeli politicians have shown themselves to a large degree to be pragmatic (notwithstanding ideological stances), adaptive, internally competitive, and fairly moderate.[14] Coalition government has in any case limited the power of the largest party,[15] and Israeli politics have evolved on the basis of a fairly well-integrated and pluralistic society,[16] reflecting orderly change.[17]

Israel's experience with proportional representation tends to confirm the observation of Lakeman and Lambert that "in many cases proportional representation has produced political harmony. This is especially true of countries with a more mature experience in self-government, where there has grown up a truer understanding of democracy and an increased sentiment of national unity."[18] While the sovereign experience of West European nations has been longer than that of independent Israel, it may be recalled that Jewish parliamentary practice really began with the first Zionist Congress of 1897, so that one may argue that the Knesset had behind it, when it first convened, a full 50 years of solid experience.

An assessment of the Israeli system in the light of the factors enumerated by M. Weiner and J. La Palombara[19] indicates that political participation always has been

large and vocal. Under the Mandate, the Knesset Yisrael—
as the lay organ of the Jewish community—was based on the
principle of the full admission of any interested citizen
into the party system, a tradition continued after independence. The legitimacy of Israeli sovereignty was assured
by the Declaration of Israeli Independence, signed by delegates of all parties in the country. This historic document
formally ended the highly charged clash of interests and
personalities within the Jewish community that had threatened, on several occasions, to lead to serious consequences.
Acceptance by all of a mutually normative democratic framework, and the establishment of a coalition government based
on the ballot box, indicated the successful adoption of the
parliamentary method. Similarly, there took place a political transfer of power from David Ben Gurion to Moshe Sharett, Levi Eshkol, and later to Golda Meir within the context
of party politics, although admittedly not without a severe
internal crisis (the Lavon Affair, which led Rafi to split
away from Mapai for a few years).

Modern students have seen political parties as aggre-
gating interests, setting goals, and formalizing conflict.
To a fair degree this description fits Israeli parties today. Practically all of them represent definite economic
interests; their goals range from establishing theocracy,
through laissez-faire and a democratic welfare state, to
communism. Patronage is institutionalized in the coalition
agreements, it being understood that certain government
posts will be allotted in definite proportions to loyal members of the coalition parties. An Israeli political scientist has described this as a "neofeudal" system, implying
that the relationship of party to member/voter was like
that between baron and vassal.[20] This characteristic,
which was strong before and immediately after independence,
is now very much in decline, as bureaucratization and an
increased stress on universalistic norms gain ground. The
party having actively assisted the immigrant, through the
Jewish Agency, in coming to and settling down in Israel
(then Palestine), he was in return expected to owe his allegiance to it. With the attainment of independence and
the transfer of many functions held by parties—either directly or through the Histadrut and Jewish Agency—to the
state, there has been a corresponding decline in the neofeudal character of Israeli parties. A survey of the various aspects of government shows that depoliticization, or
bureaucratization, has taken place at different speeds in
different areas. The judiciary, it is generally accepted,
is above and outside party politics in Israel. The army,

following Ben Gurion's decisive action in abolishing party "private armies," also has retained its nonparty role, owing absolute allegiance to the civilian government.[21] Following intense debates in the Knesset, education has been largely depoliticized. In the civil service, there is an increased emphasis on enrollment and promotion by merit, not by party affiliation; and the only remaining strongholds of party control affecting the daily life of the citizen are the Histadrut-run health service, available only to union members, and the Rabbinical courts and offices, which are staffed by members or supporters of the religious parties. Today it would be a gross exaggeration to talk of neofeudalism in Israel. Agrarian, commercial, industrial, and other economic interests in the government and Histadrut-run sectors are linked deviously with party coalition arrangements. The individual member of a party is less dependent today than in the past on his party for economic status; he is more free to express dissent at the polls, or by use of the strike through workers' action committees, which may not necessarily enjoy the backing of the party-directed, Histadrut-affiliated trade union to which he formally belongs. As Israel develops toward a free and open society, the neofeudal ties of the past are crumbling, and the political result may be a rise in the mobile, or floating vote, in coming elections. (It is estimated that 20 to 32 percent of the Jewish voters in Israel are members of some political party.)[22]

Israeli parties maintain small staffs of professionals who earn their living directly from party politics. As noted by Jupp, in competitive party systems, politics is still the province of amateurs. In Israel this is particularly obvious during election campaigns, when party staffs are swelled by the addition of extra propagandists, speakers, writers, organizers, and so on, who between elections are normally engaged in such low-key party functions as participating in party meetings or reading party literature.

Following Jupp's classification of parties into ideological, programmatic, and adjustive, one may discern a slow but steady shift--covering the last 50 years--of Israeli parties away from revolutionary ideology, through programmatic postures (prevalent today), to the essentially conservative adjustive position (Jupp's definitions).

The only self-styled "revolutionary" groups in Israel today are extreme left-wing sects, such as Matspen or Siach, not yet represented in the Knesset, whose articulation stands in inverse ratio to their size and importance. All the labor parties as well as the independent liberals,

Herut, and the socialist-religious groups may be defined as "programmatic." The emergence of Herut from a guerrilla underground of prestate revolutionaries into a responsible parliamentary party--which between 1967 and 1970 even joined the coalition--is an instance of such far-reaching change. The remaining parties, which today include the extreme ortho dox and the capitalist-oriented Liberals (former General Zionist), are essentially conservative in character. Among the socialists, claims are heard sometimes that Labour it-self is becoming an "adjustive," or even a conservative party. The abortive "rebellion" of Histadrut Secretary Ben-Aharon in 1973 was not unrelated to this concept. The state, or national bodies such as the Jewish Agency and the Histadrut, provide most services required by the citi-zen. Party activity therefore has been channeled at times to secure that part of the national cake that could attract voters. Class consciousness was not very well developed in a country where the wage ratio between cabinet ministers and the people who clean their offices used to be not more than four to one.* The fundamental equality of Israeli society (relatively speaking) is one in which the average yearly income per capita is $1,600 and the vast majority of the people are lower middle class. Although Israel does have poverty, this, too, is only relative (when compared, say, to India); and one could have compared, in 1973, Is-rael with France or Italy in terms of standards of living. Israel has no tradition of an ancient aristocracy; the bib-lical "caste" division into priesthood (cohen, levy) and laity (israel) is confined today only to certain religious rituals and is economically meaningless. The trade unions of Israel were kept (at least until 1973) strongly progov-ernment and were not generally amenable to the ideas of class war. All these factors have tended to take the wind out of the sails of Marxism in Israel, and there has been a slow but steady shift to the right in public opinion the past few years. A general shift to the right in the ideo-logical positions adopted by many Israeli voters has been noted in interviews, despite an apparent consistency in vot-ing behavior. Least reflective of this shift are the mem-bers of the Knesset themselves, whose professed views most closely resemble their actual voting patterns.[23]

---

*Nevertheless, a small, but evident, prosperous class has risen up in recent years, which is enjoying a standard of living that already has provoked social unrest.

The steady decline in the importance of agriculture, the growing industrialization of Israel's cities using highly skilled labor (for example, in electronics), and the development of a consumer society are fast creating a situation in which the time-honored socialist ideologies--the official raison d'etre of Israel's main parties--of the past 50 years must adapt to new conditions. Classical Zionism emphasized the return to the soil, often mystically so. The ideal of the pioneer included the scholar who left his books in order to plow the land. Similar ideas are found in contemporary Maoism. The city on which the early Zionist pioneers turned their backs in disdain was inhabited by parasites, or to use a more famous epithet, by the petit bourgeois. Yet, in modern Israel it is precisely the humble town-dweller who constitutes the vast majority of the nation.[24] Urban concentration is characteristic today of all countries and continents; and the pioneering values of Israel's tomorrow will have to be redefined in an urban context, as unromantic as it may seem to ancient ideologies of veteran _kibbutz_ farmers. In the prestate days, political parties successfully carried out a major national role in promoting agricultural settlement in mountain and desert and in friendly competition laid the infrastructure of village communities, which was assumed to be of vital strategic importance in defining the frontiers of Israel. Yet today, the frontiers are defended not by the private armies of political parties but by a regular national army. Agriculture has become just another specialized, and rationalized, venture of economics. Israeli parties are indeed at the stage where pioneering values and slogans, cherished for so long, must be reexamined honestly to meet the new urban technological challenge. Israel today is more conurbation than _kibbutz_.

The impact of television on politics has been noted in many lands. The silver screen of television reached Israel with some delay. It was used initially during the 1969 Knesset election campaign. Attendance at party rallies may be expected to drop in future elections due to the prevalence of television sets. Meanwhile, the need to canvass members for donations may be lessened drastically by recent Knesset legislation that ensures that election expenses of parties, within prescribed budgets, will be defrayed by the national exchequer. One may predict the eventual limitation of party roles to the specific electoral function; indeed, it would appear today that the Israeli party is much less of a movement than it was in preindependence days. It is an institution, and as such displays all the symptoms of

31

organizational maladies known to Northcote Parkinson. To
fight elections and bargain over the results in terms of
coalition agreements has become the major occupation of any
Israeli party of whatever hue.

Many of the changes needed in Israeli political life
have perforce been delayed by the abnormal relationship of
Israel and her neighbors. So far, not one Arab state, after
many decades of conflict, has signed a peace treaty with Israel; vast human, spiritual, intellectual, economic, and
other resources have had to be deflected to defense on both
sides of the hostile borders, resources that could have been
put to better and more lasting use. The eventual easing of
tensions, leading perhaps to normal international relationships among the states of the Middle East, would pose a new
set of challenges not only to Israeli political thinkers
and leaders but also to their Arab counterparts. Recent
years, particularly since the wars of 1967 and 1973, show
a proliferation of ideas among various Israeli political
circles and the growth of a lively debate concerning the
shape of the peace to come. However, these exercises still
are regrettably rather academic; but it is possible that
the new pioneering ethic, the slogans of tomorrow sought by
Israeli political thinkers, will be found in the context of
a meaningful and mutually desirable relationship with the
Arab world. Desert wastes, hunger, thirst, illiteracy,
poverty, and disease are no strangers to the Middle East.
The challenge is there; it remains to be seen whether the
proper response will come.

The Geneva Conference, following the Yom Kippur Arab
assault on Israel and the carnage of the battlefield, may,
if successful, be the first step in this direction.

The alternatives range from the sterile perpetuation
of unhappy strife to a global nuclear catastrophe; but the
entire subject is outside the scope of this book.

NOTES

1. D. Ben Gurion, "Israel Among the Nations," Government Yearbook (Jerusalem: Israel Government Press, 1952),
p. 4.

2. G. C. Hurewitz, Middle East Politics--the Military
Dimension (New York: Praeger Publishers, 1969), p. 371.

3. See Basic Law: The Government, 1968 (Appendix 7
of present work).

4. D. Block, "The Government of Israel," Davar (daily),
April 29, 1971.

5. S. Henig, _European Political Parties_ (London: Political and Economic Press), p. 512.

6. L. D. Epstein, _Political Parties in Western Democracies_ (New York: Praeger Publishers, 1967), pp. 70-71.

7. J. Jupp, _Political Parties_ (London: Routledge and Kegan Paul, 1968).

8. Ibid., p. 10.

9. Ibid., p. 4.

10. Ibid., p. 13.

11. P. S. Bernstein, _What the Jews Believe_ (New York: Farrar, Straus, and Young, 1951), p. 419.

12. L. H. Fuchs, _The Political Behavior of American Jews_ (Glencoe, Ill.: Free Press, 1956), p. 191.

13. Ibid., pp. 124-125.

14. J. La Palombara and M. Weiner, _Political Parties and Political Development_ (Princeton, N.J.: Princeton University Press, 1968), p. 31.

15. Ibid., p. 35.

16. Ibid., p. 45.

17. G. Sartori, "Effects of Proportional Representation," ibid., p. 175.

18. E. Lakeman and J. D. Lambert, "Voting in Democracies," _Comparative Politics_, ed. H. Eckstein and D. E. Apter (New York: The Free Press, 1963), p. 282.

19. Ibid., p. 31.

20. A. Etzioni, ed., "The Decline of Neofeudalism in Israel," _Studies in Social Change_ (New York: Holt, Rinehart, and Winston, 1966), pp. 180-197.

21. A. Perlmutter, "The Israeli Army in Politics--the Persistence of the Civilian over the Military," _World Politics_ 20, no. 4 (July 1968). However, post-1973 war developments have raised some doubts.

22. E. Guttman, "Israel," _International Social Science Journal_, vol. 12 (1960).

23. A. Arian, "Voting and Ideology in Israel," _Midwest Journal of Political Science_ 10, no. 3 (1966): 265-287.

24. E. Cohen, _The City in the Zionist Ideology_ (Jerusalem: Hebrew University, 1970); and I. Galnoor, "Social Indicators and Social Planning in Israel," _State and Government_ (Hebrew) 1, no. 2 (1971); also D. Elazar, _Israel--from Ideological to Territorial Democracy_ (New York: General Learning Press Reprints, 1971).

4

THE MAJOR POLITICAL BLOCS

It is possible to classify the parties of Israel in several ways. A U.S. observer of Israeli politics has noted the following salient features of the Israeli political scene.

Broadly speaking there are three major political movements--labor, nationalist, and religious--and two minor ones--liberal and communist. Within the labor movement and indeed within the entire spectrum, Mapai maintains a dominating and central position. It would seem indeed that the nonsocialist, secular parties (referred to also as the Nationalists) are more prone to electoral change than the other two movements, whose strength is fairly stable. Within the religious movement, there is a substantial intramural competition, accompanied by pressure from secular parties interested in the evolution of patterns that would suit them. Arab politics in Israel occupy a satellite relationship within the larger party system; many Israeli parties maintain Arab "wings" through which they compete for the Arab vote. In election campaigns, Israeli parties have tended to concentrate a considerable part of their effort against opposition groups or factions closest to them within their own movements rather than against other movements.[1]

A British mathematician's analysis[2] has prompted Table 5. (A few small changes have been incorporated in his presentation to bring the table up-to-date.) A word of explanation is in order regarding the "Indeterminate" ratings given to some parties.

Herut has never made up its mind on the religious question although it tends to the proreligious side. The Independent Liberals would like to see a social welfare

TABLE 5

Political Attitudes in Israeli Parties

Name of Party	Capitalist (A), Socialist (B)	Activist (C), Nonactivist (D)	Religious (E), Secular (F)	Pro-USSR (G), Pro-United States (H)	Zionist (I), Anti-Zionist (J)	Movement
Herut	A	C	X*	H	I	Nationalist (Likud)
Liberals	A	D	F	H	I }	
Independent Liberals	X*	D	F	H	I	Liberal
Mapai (labor)	B	C	F	H	I	Socialist
Ahdut Ha'avoda	B	C	F	H	I }	
Hapoel Hamizrahi	B	D	E	H	I	
Mizrahi	A	D	E	H	I }	Religious
Agudat Yisrael	A	D	E	H	X*	
Maki	B	D	F	X*	I	
Mapam	B	D	F	X*	I }	Marxist
Rakah	B	D	F	G	J	

*Indeterminate.

35

state with free enterprise, neither wholly socialist nor capitalist. Agudat Yisrael was anti-Zionist before independence but later joined the Knesset and faces unresolved theological problems on the subject. Maki, the Israel Communist Party, and Mapam, the United Socialist Party, used to be staunch supporters of the USSR but have since been disillusioned.

Another graphic presentation of the Israeli political scene shows three concentric circles. The innermost is that of the permanent coalition members, the second that of occasional coalition partners, and the outermost that of the permanent opposition, the whole being arrayed on a socialist-capitalist horizontal axis and a secular/radical-religious vertical axis. This would indicate that the coalition tends to include the more moderate parties within each movement, while excluding the others. Variations in the composition of the coalition usually have been limited to the same elements, reshuffled from time to time.

THE LABOR MOVEMENT AND ITS PARTIES

The largest Israeli political movement is the Labour Alignment (Ma'arach), which is constituted of two parties allied together.

The Israel Labour Party, composed of
 Mapai (the dominant component)
 Ahdut Ha'avoda
 Rafi
The United Workers' Party, composed of
 Mapam

In further alliance with the Ma'arach are two Arab lists:

Progress and Development
Arab Bedouin List

In the 1973 elections, the Labour Alignment and its allies won 54 seats in the 120-seat Knesset, thus compelling the party leader, Golda Meir (of Mapai), to seek a coalition once again with partners outside the labor camp in order to obtain a working majority (see Postscript).

The History of the Israeli
Labor Movement

"Mapai and the movement it leads is distinguished by its sense of historic mission . . . to liberate the Israelis from exile, to liberate their homeland, and to liberate the Jewish working class, ensuring that Israel's development will be carried out by Jewish Labour alone."[3]

An Israeli scholar has stressed the basically revolutionary nature of Zionism as a social movement.[4] It was the crucial contribution of Zionist socialism to the Jewish renaissance to claim that Zionism could never succeed as a purely political movement but also would have to be a movement of social revolution, aimed at reshaping the social composition of the Jewish people. Jews everywhere, the familiar argument ran, were to be found in the middle or lower-middle classes; there were no Jewish peasants, no Jewish workers, very few Jewish artisans. Hence, the painful decision, not an easy one for socialists to arrive at, to bar cheap Arab labor from Jewish settlements so as not to create a white-settler, colonial-like, "European" elite living off cheap "native" labor. It surely is a paradox that it had been this insistence of the Zionist labor movement on "Jewish labor," excluding the Arab agricultural proletariat from the Jewish labor market, that saved the Jews of Palestine from the social fate of a South Africa or an Algeria. Socially, economically, and nationally, the idea of Zionism was exactly the opposite of the white-settler communities in the Third World. This effort ultimately resulted in the conscious creation of a Jewish peasantry and a Jewish working class--perhaps the most revolutionary downward mobility ever experienced in social history. It was the same conceptual framework that placed the kibbutsim and moshavim in such socially strategic positions in Israeli society and created the Histadrut not as a mere trade union organization but as a society of laborers (Hevrat Ovdim) owning industries, banks, and cooperatives and trying to coordinate a vision of social reconstitution with political aims and manipulation.

Jewish connections with socialism may be traced to the early days of that movement. In the 19th century, many persons of German-Jewish origin provided the ideological leadership for the socialist groups--such as Marx, Lassalle, and Hess. The leaders of Austrian socialism (Austro-Marxism) and Hungarian communism were almost entirely Jewish, and before World War I there was not a single non-Jew in some East European delegations to the Congress of the Second International.[5] However, only a small minority of Jews permanently aligned themselves with the party of revolution. The vast majority of European Jewry west of Russia flirted with radical politics only for a very brief period in the wake of a widespread revolutionary wave, such as before and during 1848. Only where there was no strong liberal party or where there was a threat of right-wing anti-Semitism did they give their vote to the social democrats. But a large section of European Jewry was middle class in character and supported middle-of-the-road liberal and democratic parties, somewhat left of center but not too much. These Jews were patriotic and, to a large extent, conformist; they joined a revolutionary movement only in the face of a government that oppressed them. In this decade, when the union of socialism with nationalist awakening is suddenly the great political aspiration of "progressive" people everywhere, it is surely worth noting that the Zionists were the first to articulate this program on a serious scale--and in a period when doctrinaire internationalism was vehemently professed by all other social-revolutionary groups. Radical socialist movements of the Third World and their supporters elsewhere might learn a great deal from Zionism--if they were not so busy denouncing it.

In Russia under the czars, young Jewish intellectuals were swept up in the revolutionary fervor that was to lead to the eventual overthrow of the royal house and its replacement by communism. In idealistic fashion, many Jews believed that as an educated minority in Russia it was their duty to help reform, or replace, what was agreed by all to be a reactionary and oppressive regime. Jewish socialist and communist groups arose, reflecting in their diversity the variety of revolutionary views held by their Russian contemporaries. At the same time, Zionist groups, influenced by leading Jewish intellectuals, called for a specifically Jewish revolution outside and beyond the Russian context. Between the two wings, which argued fervently about the future role of the Jewish people, there came into being a Jewish Zionist-socialist movement, which gained in strength as it realized that the Russian socialist revolution did not hold out hope for the Jews as Jews. The October Revolution of 1905, which ended in massacres of Jews by revolutionaries and counterrevolutionaries alike, spurred a young group of Jewish idealists to leave Russia and travel to what was then the Ottoman Empire to settle down in the ancient Jewish homeland and to seek socialism in a Jewish context.

Despite the relatively tiny number of people involved in this early pioneering immigration, many groups and parties, or rather nuclei of social movements, arose. In their ideological disputes as well as to some extent in their personal relationships, most of these immigrants exhibited all the sectarian intensity and exclusiveness of extreme social movements. In spite of their common aims, each believed that it had the unique solution to all major problems; and the various groups' antagonism toward each other was only somewhat mitigated by the fact that all of them were dependent on external resources for the realization of their common aims and therefore were forced to act within the common framework of the Zionist Organisation. This essential cooperation in turn helped to shape the federative nature of the Zionist Organisation and to legitimize the coalition-based governments of the future State of Israel.

The young men and women who traveled from Russia to the swamps and deserts of Israel in the first decade of the 20th century regarded themselves as pioneers, in the revolutionary concept of the avant-garde, or in Hebrew, _halutz_. The slogan of pioneering, _halutziut_, embraced for them a national, economic, socialist, and cultural revival of the Jewish people.

For practical as well as ideological reasons they lived frugally and ascetically. They stressed such values as dedication to the good of the community, equality, the sharing of property, the application of brain and brawn to the conquest of the desert, and they strove to live up to their noble ideals. Their ideology of rebellion against their elders, their dissociation from adult society (many were teen-agers), and the migratory character of their movement allowed them to realize their ideal society in geographically inhospitable, and consequently empty, regions of swamp and desert in what was then Palestine. The local Arab farmers who shunned such areas thought that the young "Moskobi," as Russian Jews were called by them, were quite mad.

David Ben Gurion[6] eloquently describes his own feelings upon arriving from Russia at Jaffa Port in 1906 at the age of 19.

We had left behind our books and our theorising, the hairsplittings and the arguments, and come to

the land to redeem it by our labour. We were
still fresh, the dew of our dreams was still
moist in our hearts; the blows of reality had
still to sober our exalted spirit.

Ben Gurion and his friends had been inspired by the
Workers of Zion (Poalei Zion) movement in Minsk, Russia,
which in 1904 published its manifesto[7] in which it declared:

We want to establish a home for all the Jewish
people . . . had we thought that the Russian revolution would solve the Jewish problem, that is
if we were to think that all the troubles of the
Jews of Russia were due only to Czarist tyranny,
then we would not be Zionists. But we are convinced that the revolution here cannot solve the
Jewish problem.

The young Jewish pioneers, short of funds but high in
spirit, deliberately forgot that they were college graduates
or students and hired themselves out as manual laborers to
the veteran Jewish community. Putting socialist theories
into immediate practice they took to forms of labor organization and agitation that were quite unknown in the feudal
Ottoman/Arab economy. Palestinian Arab peasants and feudal
landlords did not take kindly to these developments, compelling the young settlers to establish their own self-
defense organization, the Watchman (Hashomer) in 1909. In
the same year they organized themselves into work battalions
(gdudei avoda), which undertook assignments on a cooperative
basis. Part of the income was pooled in a common fund
called the Land of Israel Workers' Fund. Hashomer became
a militant left-wing nucleus inside the Zionist movement,
and by 1919 it was no longer a watchmen's society but a
revolutionary and socialist political cadre, having considerable influence on later political and military developments.[8] One of the exponents of socialist Zionism, Berl
Katznelson (editor of the Histadrut daily Davar), proposed
in 1920 to unite the various rival socialist Zionist movements in a federation of trade unions. Although Katznelson
was against the politicization of trade unions, he was
forced to concede that this was inevitable.[9] At its foundation in 1920, the General Federation of Labour (Histadrut)
had less than 5,000 members in a Jewish population of
100,000 living under difficult socioeconomic conditions.
It therefore undertook to create a working class by immigration, training, building up industry and agriculture,

and providing social services, besides engaging in basic trade unionism.

The growing emphasis in favor of national pioneering and colonizing created the conditions necessary for the predominance of the labor movement. Within Zionism the labor bloc attained strength when Ben Gurion became chairman of the Jewish Agency in 1935. Since then the Israeli people have been led by Labour. The Vaad Leumi (National Council) correspondingly declined in importance. The ideological stance was adjusted accordingly: the labor movement claimed that it fought not just for the working class but for the entire Jewish nation. In fact it came to consider itself the very nucleus of the nation.[10]

The Israeli sociologist S. Eisenstadt has noted the essentially political character of the Histadrut from its very beginning. Most of its economic and labor activities were shaped by political considerations, which were seen in a national perspective. Membership in the labor movement and adherence to its collective symbols became eventually basic prerequisites for the allocation of jobs or funds. In the political arena, membership in the labor movement became a prerequisite for accession to elite position and for political status.[11]

An ideologist of the World Labour Zionist Movement, S. Derekh, has noted:

> The strength of Israeli socialism does not result
> from its relative success or failure in parliamen-
> tary elections. Its main support is not formal
> power. On the contrary, this power is itself the
> function and not the source of its strength. The
> main prop is its high degree of control of basic
> power positions in the industrial and agricul-
> tural economy of modern Israel, in marketing
> mechanisms, in the network of vital services and
> in a series of other functions which regulate the
> life of a modern state, and which are under the
> direct or indirect control of the labour movement.
> Israeli socialism never underestimated the impor-
> tance of political institutions, but neither did
> it regard them as the sole, or even the main re-
> pository of actual power. Israeli socialism has
> always known that power means not only a majority
> of the electorate and of parliament (which as
> noted it has not yet attained); it understood
> that, in addition to it, power is comprised of an
> extremely variegated network of institutions

wielding decisive influence, the basis of which
are the key positions in the economy and in the
larger institutional sectors of society such as
education, culture, mass communications, etc.
It has learnt from its own experience and that
of others that only the combination of all aspects of power including, of course, the purely
political one, can safeguard the political and
social hegemony of the working class and its
leadership in the State. Only when political
power rests on the many non-political positions
of strength, is it guarded against the danger
of becoming an object which passes from hand to
hand with the change in the parliamentary majority, as has happened elsewhere.[12]   [Emphasis
added.]

Israel is the only country in the world that has na-
tionalized over 95 percent of the land and 100 percent of
the natural resources in democratic fashion and by legal
means. This has simplified considerably the problem of
land reform as far as Israel is concerned. Electricity,
rail services, heavy industry, ports and aviation, shipping,
and public transport are all owned by the public sector,
state or cooperative. The same is true of all water resources. Labor ownership controls 75 percent of agricultural production, 25 percent of industrial production, 20
percent of banking, and 45 percent of building construction.
Israel's economy is therefore partly public and partly
private, having about half of all the enterprises and resources under public control. The veteran Indian leader
Acharya J. B. Kripalani observed, following a visit to
Israel:

Israel has a great lesson to teach, especially the
underdeveloped countries of Asia and Africa. It
is that revolutionary social construction on an
egalitarian basis, free from exploitation, can be
effected without recourse to violence and without
dictatorship or impairing the freedom of the individual. It can be accomplished on the moral basis of justice, fair play, and neighbourly cooperation.[13]

The Growth of the Labor Movement

In April 1911, the Conference of Jewish Workers in
Galilee elected a committee of seven, including Berl Katz-

42

nelson, who took part later that year in the Conference of Jewish Workers in Judea. By 1914, Katznelson was acknowledged as a leader of Jewish labor. Since he immigrated in 1909 from Russia, Katznelson, joined by Ben Gurion and others, was a major exponent of labor unity. In 1916 the first such attempt was made, but the battles between the British and Turks during World War I prevented the holding of the planned convention of labor.

In March 1918, after the defeat of the Turks, the Conference of Jewish Workers in Judea met again, led by Katznelson, who urged mass immigration, fast development of the economy, and the allocation of land to the Jewish tiller. There were already two Jewish labor parties, both founded in 1905. Poalei Zion (Zionist Workers) and Hapoel Hatsair (Young Workers) agreed on essentials, but, whereas Poalei Zion was linked to a party of the same name in Russia, its rival was more independent. (David Ben Gurion was a member of Poalei Zion, while Katznelson regarded himself as non-party, but close to Poalei Zion.)

The numbers involved were extremely small. The total number of Jewish workers in Palestine in 1906 was 550, of whom 200 were members of the Jewish trade unions. Of the 350 immigrants from Russia, half or more did not belong to any party, so that in 1906 Hapoel Hatsair had a total membership of 90 and Poalei Zion, 60. By 1910, Poalei Zion reached 200 members. Most Jewish workers immigrating during that period refrained from joining either party as they saw in the rivalry an artificial and irrelevant feature. Katznelson became their spokesman and in 1918 opened discussions with Ben Gurion and Ben Zvi (later to become president of Israel), which led to joint party elections for a Farm Workers' Conference, in which 58 seats were divided between Poalei Zion (19), Hapoel Hatsair (11), and the non-party group (28). Katznelson, who gave the keynote speech, called for the expansion of the conference to include urban as well as rural labor, and to encourage participation of the free professions. Warning against narrow dogmatism, Katznelson sought to broaden the base of labor unity. By the end of the conference, Katznelson and Ben Gurion were able to declare the establishment of the Unity of Labour Movement (Ahdut Haavoda), which was to embark immediately upon an activist program of socialism, development, and nationalist unification. Despite a split in Poalei Zion (Europe) in Vienna, 1920, between pro- and anticommunist Zionists, the labor movement in Palestine went ahead with the establishment of the General Federation of Labour (Histadrut), in which 4,433 workers elected 38 Ahdut Haavoda

members to an assembly of 87. Hapoel Hatsair, which contested separately, won 27 seats; the New Immigrants Party,
16; and the procommunist wing of Poalei Zion (later to
evolve into the Israel Communist party), 6 seats. Katznelson reiterated his belief in the inadvisability of having
so many parties in such a small community and emphasized
his doctrine of labor unity. In the same year, elections
were held for the First Elected Assembly of the Jewish Community. Apart from Agudat Israel's supporters, 77 percent
of those eligible to vote out of a total electorate of 28,755
took part. The 314 seats were apportioned thus: 111 for
all Labour parties (70 seats for Ahdut Ha'azoda and 41 seats
for Hapoel Hatsair); 67 seats were divided between 10 other
small lists, the largest being the Farmers' List with 16;
a coalition of Religious parties won 64 seats (20 percent
of the vote); and four Sephardi communal lists won an ag-
gregate of 82 seats (23 percent).* The Labour parties were
the strongest bloc from the beginning with 45.4 percent.

By 1921 Katznelson felt strong enough to challenge the
other two major Zionist groups, the General Zionists (Weizmann) and the Mizrahi (religious), for control of the world
Zionist movement. Repeated clashes within the Zionist con-
gresses during the 1920s led eventually to the establishment of a strong labor representation within the world
Zionist movement. In 1927, Katznelson wrote to a friend:
"Our failures so far must impel us to conquer the Zionist
movement." In 1925 Katznelson became editor of <u>Davar</u>,
the General Federation of Labour daily newspaper, and he
used his editorial position to great advantage. By 1930 he
was able to influence the parties of Ahdut Ha'avoda and
Hapoel Hatsair to unite formally in Mapai--Mifleget Poalei
Eretz Yisrael (Workers of the Land of Israel Party). Taking advantage of a split in the General Zionist movement,
Mapai was able within a few years to obtain leadership of
the Zionist Congress. Within the party, Ben Gurion, who
had worked for many years with Katznelson, became the (almost) undisputed party leader, remaining virtually unchal-
lenged with the death of Katznelson in 1944.[14]

The Israel Labour Party

The largest Israeli party today is the Israel Labour
Party (Mifleget Ha'avoda Hayisraelit), founded in January

---

*This essentially conservative combination of 43 percent
has rarely maintained its unity, and its factions have alternated ever since these early elections between partnership with Labour and opposition to it.

1968 by the union of Mapai (established in 1930), Ahdut
Ha'avoda-Poalei Zion (founded, 1944), and Rafi, the Israel
Labour List (which broke away from Mapai in 1965). The
relationships among the three groups, which have retained
their identities as blocs within the united party, have
still not been determined finally and may yet give rise to
new political patterns in Israel.

The Israel Labour Party is a member of the Socialist
International. Other socialist parties of the same international organization that were in power, or in coalition,
in 1969 included the Belgian Socialist Party, the Finnish
Social Democratic Party, the German Social Democratic Party,
the Italian Socialist Party, the Labour Party of Britain,
the Icelandic Social Democratic Party, the Madagascar Social
Democratic Party, the Mauritius Labour Party, the San Marino
Independent Social Democratic Party, the Singapore People's
Action Party, the Swedish Social Democratic Labour Party,
and the Swiss Social Democratic Party.

The major component of the Israel Labour Party is
Mapai, which is a federation of groups. The major ones are
Ihud Hakvutzot Vehakibbutzim, an organization of collective
settlements in which about 97 percent of the population vote
for Mapai; an organization of cooperative villages, Tnuat
Hamoshavim, with about the same ratio of support; the Histadrut group; professionals and intelligentsia; Mapai members
in government administration; and representatives of new immigrant groups. A major faction inside Mapai is known colloquially as the Gush (bloc), representing the labor unions
of the Tel Aviv region. A competing bloc exists among the
labor unions of Haifa, centered around the port and the har-
bor industries, the third urban base being Jerusalem.

The second component of the Israel Labour Party, Ahdut
Ha'avoda, was founded in 1919 in its original form, at Petach
Tiqva near Tel Aviv. It merged with the rival Hapoel Hatsair in 1930 to form Mapai, but broke away again during
World War II. Ahdut Ha'avoda has a strong kibbutz base and
demanded its proper representation in the Histadrut and
future government of Israel. Its military wing, the Palmach,
commanded by General Yigal Allon (today deputy prime minister) won distinction in the 1948 War of Independence. Ahdut Ha'avoda combined with Mapam for the first two Knesset
elections but split in 1954. In 1965, Ahdut Ha'avoda joined
Mapai in the Labour Alignment. Largely at the insistence
of the late Levi Eshkol, Ahdut Ha'avoda agreed to join in
founding the Israel Labour Party.[15]

Mapam, an abbreviation of Mifleget Hapoalim Hameuhedet
(the United Workers' Party), founded in 1948, also is
closely connected with a kibbutz group based on a youth
movement (Hashomer Hatsair). Ideologically it is the most

left-wing of the Israel Labour Alignment, and it has not joined the Labour Party. Until the Stalinist anti-Jewish trials and purges of 1951-53 it was strongly pro-Soviet, but since has shown signs of disillusionment with Russia.

Under the leadership of David Ben Gurion, Rafi, an abbreviation of Reshimat Poalei Yisrael (Israel Labour List), broke away from Mapai in 1965 in the wake of an internal struggle for power that rocked the Labour movement known as the Lavon Affair.* Ben Gurion was joined by Moshe Dayan, Shimon Peres, and others. Rafi lasted as an independent party for only two years, after which most of its members, except Ben Gurion and a few of his friends, rejoined the Labour Party. Ben Gurion subsequently retired to Kibbutz Sde Boker to write his memoirs and resigned his seat in the Knesset.

The organizational structure of the Labour Party is as follows. The highest authority is the party Congress. Between sessions of Congress the party is guided by the Central Committee, which meets once every three months. It has 439 members. The Secretariat, with 189 members, is responsible for executing the Central Committee's decisions. It discusses and decides on all party matters, elects the standing committees, and sets their authority and terms of reference. The party Bureau prepares the Secretariat's agenda and is responsible for implementation of its decisions, discusses and decides matters that the Secretariat authorizes it to deal with as well as implements organizational and financial matters, discusses and decides on questions of procedure, and executes its decisions through departments that operate in the central headquarters (organization, youth, information, immigrant associations, labor unions, municipalities, and so on). The party secretary general and deputies are elected by the Secretariat. The party Court has 31 members and is elected by the Central Committee. It brings up for the approval of the committee proposals for changes in procedural bylaws when needed and sits in judgment on questions of irregularities brought by the party against a member or members and vice versa. The party Controller's Office, numbering 51 members, is elected

---

*The Lavon Affair was an internal political controversy within Mapai that arose from the failure of an Israeli military operation in Egypt; the ensuing disputes about responsibility for the operation and the importance of determining civilian command over security affairs caused Ben Gurion, P. Lavon (defense minister), and Eshkol (later Prime Minister) to differ sharply, ending in Ben Gurion's break with Mapai.

by the Central Committee. It is empowered to investigate administrative and financial procedures within the party.

All the Labour parties engage in extensive publication activity. Davar, the Histadrut daily, serves as a platform for the Israel Labour Party, the policies of which are also frequently expressed in the Jerusalem Post. Mapai publishes newspapers for immigrants in French, Rumanian, Yiddish, Polish, Hungarian, and English. Mapam publishes the Al Hamishmar daily in Hebrew. Lamerhav, the Ahdut Ha'avoda daily, recently closed down for financial reasons.

The Israel Labour Party is connected also with the World Labour Zionist Movement founded in 1968. It has branches in the Jewish communities of the United States, Canada, Latin America, Iran, Australia, and nine countries of Western Europe. The women's organization, Pioneer Women, has branches in 12 countries. Jewish youth movements are organized through the World Labour Zionist Students' Group and other organizations, active in North and South America, Europe, and Australia. The World Labour Zionist Movement has its headquarters in Tel Aviv and is administered jointly by the Israel Labour Party and its overseas colleagues.[16]

An Israeli scholar[17] has noted the relevance of the observations made by R. Michels (Political Parties) regarding the development of large labor parties in general to the specific case of the Israel Labour Party in its present form. The growing party machine has become almost an end in itself, rather than a means. Local politicians, having risen thanks to their skills in manipulation, now appear to be the most likely candidates for the succession to party leadership, as vacancies inevitably appear due to old age, sickness, and death. Today, the Bureau of the Labour Party numbers 27 members, of whom 18 are from Mapai, 5 from Ahdut Haavoda, and 4 from Rafi. Whereas the Ahdut Haavoda and Rafi members are largely leaders of their groups, the Mapai contingent is made up mainly of "organization men," originating principally in the party "machine" of the Tel Aviv metropolitan area, the Gush. Only 14.7 percent of the Bureau members have university educations, and the general tone appears to be nonintellectual. As the dominant body within the leader of the government coalition, the party Bureau may be expected to have a profound influence on the future development of Israel, particularly in the internal political sphere, although it may be expected also to express its opinions, at least, on practically every other subject affecting national policy. (Following the 1973 War, a new group emerged in the Labour movement calling

47

itself Etgar--the Challenge. It was composed of retired
generals who declared they would work for reforms from
within.)

THE NATIONALIST PARTIES

The nonsocialist, secular parties in Israel are divided
into two groups:

    The Likud Union, composed of
        Herut Party } formerly the "Gahal bloc"
        Liberal Party }
        Free Centre (ex-splinter of Herut)
        State List (ex-Rafi)
        Movement for the Land of Israel
    The Liberal Knesset bloc, composed of
        Independent Liberal Party
        Civil Rights Movement

Within the Likud, the Herut and Liberal Parties were joined
since 1965 as the Gahal bloc. For the sake of convenience,
the Likud Union may be said to resemble the British Conser-
vatives or the U.S. Republicans in background and outlook,
while the Liberal bloc is closer to the British Liberals or
the U.S. Democratic Party.

All these parties advocate the ideals of human freedom,
democratic government, and a free enterprise economy. While
staunchly Zionist, they do not identify Zionism with socialism.

The Gahal bloc was formed in 1965 as a counterbalance
to the moves for unity within the Labour movement. In 1967,
in the face of threats of war from the U.A.R., Gahal joined
the National Unity Cabinet under Prime Minister Eshkol; it
left it in 1970. The Independent Liberal Party has almost
consistently been a member of the coalition.

The Herut (Freedom) Party is descended from a political movement founded by Ze'ev Vladimir Jabotinsky, a Russian Jewish Zionist, during World War I.[18] He was convinced
that Jewish independence was conditional upon the existence
of a Jewish military force, an idea that was to be adopted,
with some modifications, by the left-wing Hashomer, Palmach,
and Hagana forces under Histadrut control. Jabotinsky supported and obtained the establishment of Jewish forces that
fought with the Allies against the Turks, but he was arrested by the British in 1920 when he tried to use these
Jewish-troops-in-British-uniform to defend Palestine Jewry
from Arab attacks.

48

After his release from jail in 1921, he formed the
Beitar youth movement as a paramilitary Jewish organization.
In Paris in 1925 he founded the International Union of Revisionist Zionists, which aimed at reviving Herzl's idea
of obtaining international recognition of Jewish sovereignty.
At the 17th Zionist Congress held in Basle in 1931 his group
won 21 percent of the vote, and his idea of intensive agricultural colonization was accepted as part of the Zionist
policy. In his demand for the immediate establishment of
the Jewish State on both banks of the River Jordan, Jabotinsky clashed both with the British mandatory rulers and with
the gradualist Zionists of the labor movement, as well as
with the Arabs of Palestine. Declaring the incompatibility
of Zionism and socialism, Beitar left the Zionist Organisation in 1934.

During World War II, Beitar was reorganized into the
National Military Organisation (NMO--Irgun Tzvai Leumi, or
Etzel), which conducted a sporadic guerrilla war against
the British and the Arabs, who were already organized into
terrorist gangs by the Mufti of Jerusalem, Haj Amin al-
Husseini. It rarely coordinated its actions with the Hagana,
which had decided to join forces temporarily with the British against the Nazis and to postpone the national struggle
against Britain until after World War II was ended and the
Nazis were defeated.

Menachem Begin, a Polish Jew who had been imprisoned
by the Communists in Poland for his Zionist activities, was
allowed to join the Polish army contingents that arrived
in the Middle East on the Allied side. He left his unit
and crossed the border to Palestine. Here, he joined the
NMO, where he succeeded Jabotinsky as leader of the movement. To Begin, the biggest disgrace of the Jewish people
was its defenselessness, which was a standing invitation
to all its enemies to commit massacre.

The traumatic news of the butchery by the Nazis of 6
million Jews in Europe shocked the Jewish world. To the
militants of the NMO it was the signal for action. Begin
called for immediate rebellion against Britain. As the
horrors of the concentration camps were revealed by Allied
forces in 1945, all sections of the Jewish community joined
in the demand for immediate independence, which was formally declared in 1948.

The NMO as well as the other paramilitary groups--the
Hagana, the Palmach, and the Israel Freedom Fighters (Lehi)
--all were disbanded by order of Ben Gurion in 1948. Their
members either joined the Israel Defence Forces, which by
agreement were to be kept (successfully) entirely outside

party politics, or reverted to civilian life, including party politics.

The ex-members of the NMO who turned to politics founded the Herut Party led by Menachem Begin.[19] Herut has been in the opposition, except for 1967-70, and has won considerable support from new immigrants. It still professes a strongly nationalistic line.

The Liberal Party of today has its antecedents in the General Zionist Movement. The party was founded in 1931 in Basle, its Palestinian branch joining in Zionist development on a nonsocialist basis. It has attracted support from the business community, and its main platform is free trade and constitutional democracy. The main center of the party is in the city of Tel Aviv. The Liberal Party has alternated between coalition and opposition. A splinter group broke away in 1948, rejoining in 1961 and leaving again in 1965. This is known as the Independent Liberal Party, historically the heir to the Progressive Party, which in turn was derived from the Aliyah Hadasha (New Immigrants) Party formed by German refugees in 1942 and the Zionist Workers Party (Haoved Hatzioni) founded in 1936 as the labor wing (Faction A) of the General Zionists.

The Independent Liberal Party (ILP), now represented by two ministers in the Cabinet, is the classic middle-of-the-road party. It strives for a social welfare state with fullest democracy and protection of the rights of the individual and attempts to exercise a moderating influence on the socialist-religious coalition of which it is a member. Opposed to extremism of all sorts, the ILP objects to the attempts of labor to make Israel a socialist state and the attempts of the religious parties to make her into a theocracy. It also believes that the powers of the Histadrut should be curtailed and that party politics be divorced from both trade unionism and religion. In its foreign policy the ILP generally supports the government.

The Civil Rights movement was founded in late 1973 and successfully contested the Knesset elections (see Postscript).

THE RELIGIOUS PARTIES

One of the central issues in Israeli political life, which not even the pressing external security problem has been able to overshadow, is the place of past tradition and ancient jurisprudence, centered on the Jewish religion, in the national fabric of a modern and secular republic.

The broad measure of national agreement on foreign policy, defense, and economics is regrettably not extended to this issue of religion. The growing militancy of the religious sector, particularly its youth, on the one hand, and that of a small but vocal secular and anticlerical group, on the other, tends to give the impression of a degree of polarization. This is in strong contrast to most Jewish communities outside Israel, where a broad consensus in favor of some type of religious continuity is to be found. No Jewish community outside Israel is politically sovereign. Such communities are all in the status of a minority within a larger, non-Jewish culture and so have never faced the question. In Israel approximately two-thirds of the population have loosened their religious ties in the sense of observance of the 613 precepts of Judaism and the many customs, rituals, and prayers of the religion. The other third (the figure is approximate) retains its devotion to this tradition, often meticulously, and is not at all happy about the increasing secularization of the majority, a process that it fears eventually may endanger the unity of the Jewish people. The existing modus vivendi between the two sectors of the public has been the subject of coalition bargaining and agreements between secular socialists and religious politicians. Yet this is an oversimplification. Just as the percentage of the electorate that casts its vote for the religious parties is not a true reflection of the numerical strength of the religious sector, so the relative readiness of politicians to compromise in order to obtain pragmatic gains is not a true reflection of the tension and soul searching of many Israelis who are deeply concerned about the future cultural patterns of their country.

It is extremely tempting for many Israelis, brought up to admire modern Western political systems, to seek a constitutional or other legal separation of church and state in Israel. However, the criteria that evolved in Europe and the United States do not necessarily fit a Middle Eastern people with an originally Asian--that is, religion-oriented--way of life, despite the conscious effort to produce a modern, democratic, and free government. It is commonly held by Israeli historical tradition that it was the Jewish religion that kept the Jewish people together during its long exile, from loss of independence in 70 CE to its reestablishment in 1948. Wedded to European concepts of self-determination and national sovereignty, it produced Zionism.

Indeed, without its religious foundations, true Zionism is devoid of meaning. In principle no religious Jew can concede the legitimacy of a purely secular basis for Jewish nationhood. At best, religious Jews regard the modern Israel as only a preparatory stage for the divinely governed regime that will arise when the Messiah, the anointed descendant of David, King of Israel, will come back to Jerusalem at a date that only God knows.

Coming down from theology to practical politics, there is a gap in the Knesset that cuts across government and opposition benches. The National Religious Party in the cabinet is strongly influenced by the religious parties sitting in the opposition when matters pertaining to religion are up for discussion. The price the socialist leaders of Israel have paid for religious support in the coalition has been the periodic enactment of proreligious legislation. In some ways this has been a continuation of a legal tradition from Ottoman times. Under Turkish law, accepted by the British Mandate and later by Israel, recognition was given to religious courts of the Jewish, Moslem, and Christian communities. Israel went further and made these religious judges into state officials. In Israel today, matters of marriage and divorce are settled in a religious court, according to the faith of the parties involved (there is no civil marriage). The state caters to the religious needs of the population by financial subventions to the institutions and holy shrines of the major religions, through the Ministry for Religious Affairs and local municipal religious councils.

Already prior to World War I, various Zionist bodies supported a network of elementary Hebrew schools in Palestine. Religious Zionists aided schools that stressed religious values, while socialist Zionists through the Histadrut replaced the prophets of Israel by the prophets of Marxism. Instead of religious hymns, children were taught to sing the "Internationale." Finally, the most orthodox Jews of the Agudat Yisrael declared that anyone who sent his children to any of these schools, including those of the religious Zionists, would be excommunicated.

Modern Israel inherited this multiple education system, permitting parents to decide to which type of school (Orthodox, religious-Zionist, socialist, or general) to send their children. However, it soon became clear that overpoliticization of schoolchildren was detrimental to their education, and a reform was made under the State Education Law of 1953, which established state and religious-state education as two options for parents of school-age

children. In fact, the Agudat Yisrael continued to maintain
its orthodox institutions.

Under a law passed in 1949, the Sabbath, traditionally
the holy day of the Jewish week, and Jewish holidays were
established as official days of rest. Non-Jews of course
may observe their own festivals. Government offices and
services, the army, and other national bodies observe the
rules of the Sabbath, and their kitchens are governed by
the Orthodox Jewish dietary rules (Kashrut). In the Israel
Army, the chief chaplain to the troops holds the rank of a
brigadier.

Religious questions that are still live issues include:
the regulation of public transport on the Sabbath; the recruitment of religious boys and girls to the army; the legal
definition of a Jew (in view of a large percentage of mixed
marriages among recent immigrants); the supervision of Jewish holy places such as the Western Wall; and whether civil
marriage should be made possible for those who desire it,
or for limited categories of citizens, or at all. It should
be noted that Israel is not unique in having such groups.
Nearly all countries of Western Europe as well as the Middle East have religious parties, ranging from Christian
Democrats to Moslem Brotherhood. A common denominator of
all these religious parties is the conviction that religion
must be defended and advanced by political means.

Israel's Jewish religious parties fall, too, within
this category. They were all founded originally in Europe
in an attempt to counter the spread of Marxism among Jewish
workers; and they found allies among the veteran Jewish population of Jerusalem, which was extremely devout. Two wings
developed among the religious parties: one tried to win
over converts from the socialist camp by espousing a combination of socialist and religious values; the other rejected the Zionist concept as secular and therefore sinful.
One thereby obtains the following table:

Religious Socialists	Religious Nonsocialists	Religious Non-Zionists
Hapoel Hamizrahi	Agudat Yisrael (AY)	Neturei Karta*
Poalei Agudat Yisrael (PAY)	Hamizrahi	

---

*Guardians of the Holy City, a very small Orthodox Jew-
ish group that believes the establishment of Israel as a

Hamizrahi and Hapoel Hamizrahi have united in the National
Religious Party and, as noted, participate in coalition.
They stand for a ban of legislation that runs counter to
the Bible and support the advancement of religious education. Founded in 1956, Hapoel Hamizrahi continues its separate existence as a trade union, to which 63 cooperative
and communal villages inhabited by religious farmers are
affiliated. The movement makes special efforts to assist
these villages in religious and other matters. The PAY and
the AY are small parties, usually in the opposition. It
is interesting to note that, in recent years, Israel's Moslems, Christians, and Druzes have not established political
movements based on religion.

THE COMMUNISTS

In Israel, Communism[20] met its match in the form of
Zionism. The very small number of Communist immigrants
who arrived from Russia found themselves in a paradoxical
situation. The small, struggling Jewish community of Palestine had very little patience for an ideology that denied
the right of the Jewish homeland to exist, banned Zionism
in Russia, exiled Jewish nationalists to Siberia or exe-
cuted them, and supported the Arabs against them. Thus,
the Communists isolated themselves from the Jewish community.

A small splinter group that broke away from Poalei
Zion in 1919 formed itself in 1920 into the Mifleget Poalim
Sozialistit (Mops--Socialist Workers' Party), but it dissolved a year later after fomenting May Day riots (January
5, 1921) leading to the death of several Jews. The Palestine Communist Party (PCP) was established in 1921, and in
1924 it was expelled from the Histadrut, where it had tried
to infiltrate. The PCP was accepted into the Comintern in
1924 and followed a pro-Arab and anti-Zionist policy of in-
citing Palestinian Arabs to attack Jewish farms. The PCP
was outlawed by the British but it continued to operate
through front organizations. When the Mufti of Jerusalem,
Haj Amin al-Husseini, embarked on his anti-Zionist policy,
the PCP offered its aid to him, but the Mufti found his

---

secular republic, without divine sanction and guidance, is
a sin. They therefore refuse to vote or pay taxes and do
not "recognize" Israel, although they live in it, mainly
in Jerusalem.

allies instead in Nazi Berlin. The PCP objected noisily to Jewish efforts to save the Jews of Germany from the growing anti-Semitism there, and when the Arabs of Palestine rebelled in 1936 against the British and the Jews, the PCP stood by them. Although most of the Jews of Palestine lived in socialist cooperative and collective farms, while the Arab Palestinian movement was backed by reactionary and feudal landlords, PCP propaganda claimed that the progressive Arabs were correctly fighting capitalist imperialist Jews, a canard that has lasted to the present--and due to sheer repetition, has had some success.

The Molotov-Ribbentrop pact naturally bewildered the PCP for a while, but soon the party fell in line and acknowledged Hitler as a friend and ally. The subsequent reversal was even easier to accept, and the PCP came out into the open, extolling the British Army. In 1947 the PCP was again taken by surprise when the Soviet delegation to the United Nations strongly supported Israel against the Arabs and when Russia extended to Israel considerable political and military assistance. The PCP had by then been acknowledged by the Arabs as a Palestinian Arab Nationalist party, with only a small number of Jewish members.

Israel has allowed the Communist Party to operate legally. In 1948, the Israel Communist Party, or Miflaga Komunistit Yisraelit (Maki) was officially founded. In 1965 it split into pro-Nasser and pro-Zionist factions, the former taking the name of the New Communist List (Reshima Komunistit Hadash--Rakah). Maki has since been openly critical of the Soviet Union, while Rakah faithfully acts on Moscow's orders. Rakah in the Seventh Knesset had three seats; Maki, one; and a fellow-traveler faction, the New Force (Koah Hadash), established by a journalist, had two seats (but this faction split in two and was defeated in the Eighth Knesset).

Most of Rakah's support comes from Israel's Arab population. An indication of Israeli democratic tolerance may be seen in the way Rakah was allowed to advertize pro-Egyptian and pro-Soviet opinions in the very midst of the October 1973 Arab onslaught.

Prior to the 1973 Knesset elections, Maki combined with new left elements to form the Moked (Focus) list, while the "New Force," also combining with new leftists, was renamed Meri (Revolt). In the 1973 elections, Meri failed to retain its seat in the Knesset, while Rakah captured half the Israeli-Arab vote.

The Communists were the only Israeli party to call for a total withdrawal of Israeli troops from all administered territories taken in 1967; Israelis who recognized the need for some territorial compromise were nevertheless wary of electing the Communists to power, a price that most voters realized was too high to pay for what seemed a very dubious peace.

NOTES

1. S. D. Johnston, "Election Politics and Social Change in Israel," Middle East Journal 16 (Summer 1962): 309-327.

2. T. M. Goodland, "A Mathematical Presentation of Israel's Political Parties," British Journal of Sociology 8, no. 3 (September 1957).

3. L. Eshkol, On the Way Up (Hebrew; Tel Aviv, 1966), quoting speech on June 30, 1962.

4. S. Avineri, "The Sources of Israeli Socialism," Israel Horizons 19, no. 3 (March 1971): 25-26.

5. W. Laqueur, "Revolutionism and the Jews," Commentary 51, no. 2 (February 1971).

6. D. Ben Gurion, Years of Challenge (New York: Holt, Rinehart, and Winston, 1963), p. 7.

7. "Poalei Zion Manifesto," Publications, Department of History (Jerusalem: Hebrew University, 1968). Translation from Yiddish to Hebrew.

8. A. Perlmutter, Military and Politics in Israel-- Nation Building and Role Expansion (London: Cass, 1969), pp. 6-9.

9. B. Katznelson, Writings (Hebrew; Tel Aviv: Mapai, no date), pp. 129, 158.

10. D. Ben Gurion, From Class to Nation (Tel Aviv: Massada, 1954), p. 379.

11. S. Eisenstadt, Israeli Society (New York: Basic Books, 1967), p. 57. An excellent introduction to Israel.

12. S. Derekh, "Israeli Socialism," pamphlet (Tel Aviv: World Labour Movement Zionist Publications, 1970), pp. 3-4.

13. Ibid., p. 38.

14. D. H. Shapiro, "A Study in Non-Institutionalised Power," State and Government 1, no. 1 (1971) (Hebrew).

15. T. Prittie, Eshkol, The Man and the Nation (New York: Pitman Publishers, 1969), p. 299.

16. Whos' Who in Israel, 1969-70 (Tel Aviv, 1971).

17. S. Weiss, "The Composition of the Israel Labour Party Bureau--An Examination and Evaluation," State and Government 1, no. 2 (1971) (Hebrew).

18. V. D. Segre, op. cit., pp. 56-57.

19. D. Ben Meir, The Character of the State of Israel (Tel Aviv: Carta, 1969), pp. 264-65; (see also Ben Meir, Crisis in Israeli Society, Carta, 1973) Leonard Fein, Politics in Israel (Boston: Little, Brown, 1967), pp. 86-89; M. Begin, The Revolt (Tel Aviv: Hadar, 1964).

20. M. Czudnowski, and J. M. Landan, The Israel Communist Party and Elections to the Fifth Knesset (Stanford: Hoover Institution, 1961); W. S. Laqueur, Communism and Nationalism in the Middle East (London: Routledge, 1957). These are the best sources on Israeli communism.

5

KNESSET AND LOCAL ELECTIONS

HOW ELECTIONS ARE HELD

Despite the constant strain imposed upon Israeli society by defense and foreign problems, not to speak of the economic and social difficulties caused by the simultaneous absorption of a million Jewish refugees from formerly Nazi-ruled Europe and the Arabic-speaking lands of Asia and Africa, together with a rapid growth in the national product, the young republic has shown consistency and vigor in the maintenance and development of democratic rule.

Israel's parliamentary elections generally are spaced at intervals of four years, but the legislature may call the electors to the polls at an earlier date, if need be.

Election day in Israel[1] brings to a climax a political campaign dominated by free speech, using all media of communication. In the concluding stages of the campaign, party spokesmen are given time, in a ratio fixed by agreement and reflecting the outgoing strengths, to state their case over the national radio and television.

For many voters, this is a unique experience. Not only new, young voters will have attained their right to vote but also between one polling day and the next, many thousands of immigrants enter Israel from many countries where democratic elections perhaps do not exist or exist only as a farce. These immigrants have the right to citizenship upon arrival and are given the vote, on an equal footing with veteran Israelis. Not surprisingly, the participation vote is usually high, over 80 percent.

Every national of Israel over the age of 18 years, man or woman, irrespective of race, creed, or former citizenship, has the right to vote. The name of everyone entitled to vote is included in the Electoral Register, which is brought up-to-date annually.

Every national of Israel who is 21 years old on the day the lists of candidates are submitted may stand for election to the Knesset, with the following exceptions:

1. holders of certain high state offices: the president, the chief rabbis, the state comptroller, and the chief of the general Staff;
2. judges of any court, including rabbinical and other religious courts;
3. officiating, salaried rabbis, priests, and other clergy;
4. regular army officers and senior civil servants, unless they resigned at least 100 days before the election.

Thus, Israel's judiciary, clergy, army, and civil service are insulated from the pressures of party politics and the turbulence of the hustings. Elections to the First Knesset were held under legislation passed for and applying to those elections only.[2] The Second Knesset Elections Law, 5711 (1951)* was intended to provide for the next elections. At the same time the law concluded with a section applying its provisions, mutatis mutandis, to the elections to the third and any subsequent Knesset, so long as no other electoral law should be adopted. The Knesset did in fact pass a new elections law in 1955, which, contrary to its ad hoc predecessors, constituted permanent legislation, though without introducing any fundamental change in the existing electoral system or process. Among the more important changes was a substantial lengthening of the periods prescribed for various electoral procedures, such as the appointment of the elections committees, the filing of objections to the Electoral Register, and the lodging of lists of candidates.

Israel's elections are "universal, nationwide, direct, equal, secret, and proportional." They are universal in the sense that all adult citizens have the right to vote. They are equal, for each citizen has only one vote. They are nationwide, the entire country (which after all is rather small) being regarded as one constituency. They are direct, since the voter casts his ballot directly for the party of his choice. They are secret: each voter, in the

---

*5711 was the year in the Hebrew, lunar calendar, and 1951 was the corresponding year in the Roman, solar calendar.

privacy of the ballot booth, places his ballot in an opaque envelope that he or she seals and, in the presence of official observers--representing as a panel the different parties contesting the vote--drops it into the ballot box. Thus, nobody can see or discover how he has voted.

The elections are proportional: the Knesset seats are allocated in proportion to the votes cast for the various parties. Each party presents a list of candidates, up to a total of 120--the entire membership of the Knesset. Most of the larger parties offer a full list of that number, some of the smaller parties offer less. The candidates on each list are set out in whatever order of priority the party itself decides. If a party were to poll 50 percent of the total valid votes cast it would get 60 out of the 120 seats. The first 60 names on that party's list would thus win seats in the House. It may be noted here that the voter has no way of selecting, or rearranging, names from a given party list when he comes to vote. It is obvious, though, that well-known candidates whose names he recognizes may stand to influence his selection of party lists. Any party receiving at least 1 percent of the total of valid votes cast may share in the distribution of seats. Parties with under 1 percent are disqualified. (This limitation clause is found in other countries with proportional representation. In Western Germany, it is 5 percent.)

There is consequently no need for by-elections to fill parliamentary vacancies caused by death or resignation, as the gap is immediately filled by the next person on the party list. For comparison with the constituency system prevailing in Britain, India, and other countries, the following table shows what would theoretically happen if four parties were to win the same proportions of the vote in Israel and Britain or India. (In the 1951 British election, Labour won most votes but lost the election! This was due of course to the system in use.[3]) In this table, as in fact, Israel is regarded as one constituency.

The Central Election Board has five major tasks:

1. setting up and supervising the Regional Election Boards, which in turn name the local Election Committees;
2. accepting the lists of candidates submitted by the parties;
3. coping with all the technical and administrative arrangements for the election;
4. policing the campaign to ensure fair play;
5. counting the ballots and certifying and publishing the results.

TABLE 6

Israeli, British, and Indian Electoral Systems-- A Theoretical Comparison

Party	Israel		A British or Indian Constituency	
	Percentage of Votes	Percentage of Seats	Percentage of Votes	Percentage of Seats
A	40	40	40	100
B	30	30	30	--
C	20	20	20	--
D	10	10	10	--

In order to regulate propaganda activities by all concerned, an amendment passed in 1959 to the Elections Law forbids entertainments to attract the public to election meetings; the use of loudspeakers, except to amplify speakers' voices at meetings; the distribution of gifts, food, or drinks in the course of electioneering; and, for a month before the election, "shots" of candidates on newsreels or television. Under the latter provision, for example, films of the prime minister's visit to the United States were not shown until after the election. Each party is entitled to 25 minutes on the state radio plus 4 minutes for every seat it held in the outgoing Knesset. There are similar arrangements for television broadcasts. These programs are of course passed by the parties themselves.

To ensure that everyone be able to vote in the place where he or she is registered, the Central Election Board organizes transport, at state expense, of electors who have moved since the qualifying date for registration or who were unable to be in their home towns on election day.

Election day itself is a public holiday and no electioneering is permitted. In army camps and outposts, polling booths, some mobile, are available. Copies of lists of candidates of all parties and manifestos are distributed to all troops, but no electioneering is allowed inside any army installation. Israeli sailors of the merchant navy, while at sea, also may vote, according to an amendment of 1969.[4] (But Israeli diplomats and other citizens abroad cannot vote, despite their legal right to do so.)

Each party is allocated a symbol composed of one or two letters of the Hebrew alphabet. This symbol appears on

all party propaganda and, on election day, on the voting
slips themselves, upon which nothing else is printed. Each
voter may take only one such slip bearing the symbol of the
party of his choice and, after sealing it, drop it in the
ballot box. If in error a voter places two or more identical slips in his sealed envelope, this will be taken as one
valid vote. The use of letters presupposes a minimal lit-
eracy; the use of pictorial symbols has not been found necessary.

The number of valid votes obtained by each party that
wins at least 1 percent of the total is divided by 120,
giving the number of seats won at this stage. Remaining
seats are allocated to the lists with the largest remainders. For example, on October 28, 1969, a total of
1,427,981 votes were cast. Deducting 60,238 invalid votes,
this gave 1,367,743 valid votes. From this total the
14,845 votes cast for the Land of Israel Party, the Peace
Party, and the Young Israel Party were deducted, leaving
1,352,898 votes. The latter divided by 120 gave a quotient
of 11,274 votes per seat. After proportionate allocation,
six seats remained unallocated, and these went to the six
lists with the largest remainders.

Israel's present electoral system has the advantage
of providing an accurate reflection of party strengths.
It is impossible for a party that has gained a minority of
the votes to win a majority of the seats. The system has
been criticized, however, on the grounds that it encourages
the growth of small parties, makes it difficult for any one
party to obtain an overall majority, and therefore necessi-
tates coalition governments. In order to participate in
the elections, a party not represented in an outgoing
Knesset must file 750 signatures of supporters and deposit
I£ 15,000 to be forfeited if no candidate is returned.[5]

Moreover, it is argued, since all candidates are nomi-
nated by party headquarters, all power is in the hands of
the parties and members of the Knesset have little independence. Since there are no constituencies, each member of
the Knesset represents a political philosophy rather than
the citizens of a particular community or locality. On the
other hand, this has had the advantage of concentrating attention on national instead of communal or local interests.

The system of proportional elections has been the subject of a fierce debate waged between a minority group in
the Knesset, which demanded a change over to the British
constituency system (plurality elections and division of
the country into several electoral districts), and the majority, which stood by the present system.

The minority, in this case, was composed of the leaders of the coalition and the opposition, Mapai and the General Zionists. The respective proposals of these two parties were not, however, identical. Mapai proposed the division of Israel into 120 constituencies, each returning one member by plurality election. Against this, the General Zionists favored a smaller number of constituencies, each returning several members by proportional election. The majority, made up of small parties from the coalition and the opposition, made certain of its victory by inserting a provision preventing the amendment of the article dealing with the electoral system except by a majority of the members of the Knesset--that is to say, on the basis of the present size of the legislature, by 61 votes.

The most vocal and insistent advocate of electoral reform, until his resignation from the Knesset, was the late Prime Minister Ben Gurion.

ELECTORAL REFORMS IN 1973

Local Government Elections

The Labour Party declared its commitment in November 1972 to enacting direct mayoral elections by the 1973 polls, over the opposition of Tel Aviv Mayor Rabinowitz, a Labour leader, who apparently was not too sure of his personal prospects in such a contest. The bill was tabled in the Knesset by ex-Rafi member Ben-Porat, and Rabinowitz was assured of his party's support in the contest with General (Res.) Lahat of Gahal for the leadership of Tel Aviv.

In March 1973, several small parties that earlier had supported the bill changed their minds in the wake of the Bader-Ofer Amendment (see Appendix C). The Knesset defeated the direct mayoral election bill on March 12, when Labour itself abandoned it because of amendments introduced by other parties requiring a 50 percent popular vote for a mayor to be elected. Prime Minister Meir stated that if the law were not struck down, with the 50 percent clause attached, "the Labour Alignment might be in danger of disappearing from the municipal map."[6]

The defunct bill was briefly resurrected by the Free Centre, with the lone support of Ben-Porat, who said "it could have facilitated the growth of a new grass-roots leadership instead of the entrenched party politicians."[7] Ben-Porat was able to reintroduce his bill again in June (without the controversial 50 percent clause), but it was blocked in committee after a first reading.[8] In May 1973, the right to vote in municipal elections was extended to the Jordanian citizens resident in the united Jerusalem municipal area.

Knesset Elections

The Labour Party dropped its proposals to raise the cutoff percentage for Knesset elections from the existing 1 percent and to increase the size of the Knesset to 150 members, due to stiff Gahal opposition. However, Labour and Gahal agreed to support a bill designed to change the distribution of surplus votes in the Knesset election. Opposing this move were eight small parties: the Agudat Yisrael, the Independent Liberal Party, the State List, the New Communists, the Poalei Agudat Yisrael, the Free Centre, Haolam Hazeh, and the Communists. The controversial amendment was jointly submitted by Y. Bader of Gahal and A. Ofer of Labour and so became known as the "Bader-Ofer Amendment.[9] This amendment to the existing election legislation was to give priority to the larger parties in the distribution of Knesset votes after the regular division of the total valid votes cast by the number of votes required per seat per party. Under the existing system a small party had a chance of winning an extra seat that proportionately gave it greater strength; Ofer said he thought this was unfair, pointing out that while no system of distributing votes ensured absolute justice the system rewarded small parties and penalized the larger ones. Gahal supported Labour apparently because, as the second largest party (albeit in the opposition), it stood to gain from the amendment.

When, on the night of January 1, 1973, the Bader-Ofer Amendment was brought for its first reading in the Knesset, the eight opposing factions launched a filibuster to prevent its passing and proposed votes of nonconfidence in the government. The debate dragged on until morning, when these motions were defeated. The bill was referred back to committee by 72 to 24 votes. Also passed in this session was the Election and Parties Financing Bill, which allowed for the subsidy by the state of all parties at elections and in the four years in between--at the taxpayers' expense. Although supported by most of the party, the Bader-Ofer Amendment was not popular with some Labour supporters.

Lea Ben Dor, the Jerusalem <u>Post</u> parliamentary commentator, observed:

> A good many people in the Alignment do not like
> the new amendment, as a bit of sharp practice un-
> becoming a self-respecting party, unnecessary,
> and liable to damage the party's image, especially
> when it was carried out arm-in-arm with the arch
> enemy, the Herut activists in Gahal. If we de-
> cide that the existence of eight small parties
> threatens the development of a stable parliamen-
> tary system, the party should say so openly and
> labour to bring in a ban.[10]

Ben-Dor concluded ruefully: "There is no reason, except sheer convenience and self-seeking, why the present constitutional change should be introduced without having been presented to the voters."

It was therefore no surprise when the authors of the amendment rejected an offer by Hebrew University mathematicians to scrutinize the fairness of the idea from a statistical standpoint.

In yet another attempt to secure an eventual Labour landslide, Deputy Transport Minister Gad Yaacobi tabled a private member's bill designed to create a new system of mixed constituency and proportional representation. The bill, however, did not get through committee.* A counter-effort by Agudat Yisrael to require a majority of 80 Knesset members for any electoral reform also was defeated.[11]

The Bader-Ofer Amendment came back on April 3 for its second and third readings amid strong opposition from the eight small parties and after an abortive attempt by the university scholars to persuade Golda Meir to withdraw her support from it. Another nightlong filibuster ensued, but the Labour-Gahal partnership bulldozed the Bader-Ofer Amendment through into law, by 75 to 20. According to this, in the 1973 elections, the size of a faction would determine the weight of its claim for an extra seat. In other words, a big party with only 500 extra votes would have a prior claim to another seat over a small party with as much as 10,000 extra votes. In a court case opened by one of the university professors against the justice minister, it was alleged that the new law would shift about 40,000 votes

---

*Yaacobi revived his bill in 1974, with the backing of the government (see Postscript).

from the small parties (for which they were cast) to the large parties.

In comparison, votes cast for a small party under the U.S. or British system are lost, and not transferred to the opposition.

FIFTY YEARS OF VOTING TRENDS (1920-70)

Study of the election results for the National Assembly of the Jews of Palestine and the Knesset elections (for polls held in 1920, 1925, 1931, 1944, and then after independence in 1949, 1951, 1955, 1959, 1961, 1965, and 1969) gives a fairly clear picture of the dominant political trends among Israel's adult population.

The labor movement—taken as a whole and ignoring its factions, incorporating all socialist groups except the communist and religious-socialist groups—rose to majority status in the 1930s, reflecting its leadership of Zionism. This lead was retained after independence until the late 1960s, when a slight drop was manifested. Labor generally had double the strength of its nearest rival, the nationalist bloc, and about three times that of the religious bloc, although this advantage slowly waned.

Within the labor movement, Mapai rose to majority rank as a party during World War II, partly because of the simultaneous withdrawal of a major element of the nationalist bloc (the revisionist-Irgun-Herut movement) from cooperation with the socialists during that critical period. When Herut returned to parliamentary life, Mapai's strength dropped, and the complementary symmetry of the labor and nationalist voting curves suggests a floating vote that moved from one bloc to the other alternately. In the 1950s, Mapai, through uniting with other socialists first in the Alignment and then in the Israel Labour Party, achieved a comeback, returning to dominate the labor movement. Nevertheless, the total strength of labor is in slow but steady decline (see Table A-7).

The nationalist bloc, comprising the Herut, General Zionists, and Progressives, rose in popularity in the 1930s, expressing nationalist feelings in the face of Nazism in Europe and (perceived) combined British-Arab hostility to the Jews in Palestine. The bloc then lost much of its parliamentary support due to the boycott of elections by the Revisionists in 1944. Following the return of the Revisionists, now renamed Herut, to the Knesset, the bloc regained its strength; but it has not yet seriously challenged the labor bloc at the national level. At local polls, the center has on occasion won municipal leadership, notably in Tel Aviv (1973).

The religious bloc also lost much of its parliamentary strength during the Mandate due to its boycott, in part, of the national Zionist institutions. After independence, nearly all religious groups accepted parliamentary norms and have been fairly consistent in maintaining about 15 percent of the vote. As noted elsewhere, their actual strength is much greater due to their coalition partnership and bargaining power.

The Communists never have risen above 4 percent, on the average, a slight rise immediately after independence being due to tactical Soviet support for Israel and a consequent ephemeral popularity of pro-Soviet attitudes in Israel, a situation that changed quickly with the transfer of Soviet support to the Arab states. Today, 20 years later, Israeli public opinion, deeply shocked by Soviet oppression of the Jews in Russia, is staunchly anticommunist. Israeli Arabs, however, form the backbone of the Israeli communist movement.

A 50-year perspective confirms the observation that the strongest bloc has been labor (the second largest, with fluctuations, the nationalists); that the religious vote is fairly stable; and that the Communists are quite incapable of overcoming their weakness in Israel.

THE FIRST KNESSET ELECTION
AFTER INDEPENDENCE

An Israeli journalist[12] who conducted his own "Gallup Poll" on the eve of the first Knesset elections has described the perplexity of the voter when confronted with a multiplicity of parties. Summarizing the platforms of the contestants, the journalist wrote that Mapai would set out not only to retain virtual control of the government but also to obtain a clear majority, on the strength of their record of the past 15 years at the helm of the Zionist movement.

The party secretary was quoted as saying that Mapai still favored a coalition government "of progressive and constructive parties." Mapai was appealing not only for the labor vote but also for the vote of the masses. An important part of Mapai's election fight was directed against Mapam and Herut. Mapam was considered to be a political rival; while Mapai's quarrel with Herut was much deeper, ideologically, as Herut opposed socialist principles.

Mapam's platform, as published in the same paper,
stressed the following points: free and unlimited immigration of Jews, agricultural settlement, planned development,
"freedom from imperialist influences," strengthening of
ties with the Soviet Union, alliance with the Arab peoples
for independence and liberation from feudalism, secularization of the state, freedom for "organs of the working
class," strict control of the economy, a "working people's
army," free education, the rescue of Jews from Arab States,
and the preservation of "socialist hegemony in a progressive government."

In contrast, Herut, the freedom movement, in an advertisement on the same page of the Palestine Post, called for
the

> consummation of the aim only partially achieved,
> the restoration of the whole Hebrew Homeland,
> east and west of the Jordan. . . . There can be
> no agreement with the invading Arab States until
> they have withdrawn their armies to within their
> own borders.

Herut defined itself as "the only true opposition within
the State." It went on to state that it was

> unalterably opposed to the prevailing system
> whereby the machinery of the State is treated by
> the various parties as the property of those par-
> ties, to be divided up according to the index of
> strength of each party . . . the basis of the
> present coalition is purely and simply an agree-
> ment on how to divide the spoils.

Herut called for constitutional guarantees of democratic
liberties and stated that it would continue to campaign for
freedom. Herut insisted on "the elimination in the first
place of any large concentration of economic power in the
hands of individuals or of groups." This was a broad hint
at the already considerable economic strength of the labor
parties.

The General Zionists, also advertising their platform,
called for "equilibrium" within the state. Noting that
labor was powerfully organized, the "growing control of the
left" was evoking a similar movement from the right. According to the General Zionists, "both are equally harmful."
In the center, it felt that businessmen, farmers, artisans,
manufacturers, professionals, and others who valued economic
and political independence should vote for its list.

The Progressive Party, in its published platform, also upheld the principles of democracy, freedom and social progress, private initiative, and cooperative effort. Quite clearly it competed for votes with the General Zionists.

The four orthodox parties--Mizrahi, Hapoel Hamizrahi, Agudat Yisrael, and Poalei Agudat Yisrael--presented a joint list. The Palestine Post commented that they had united for the elections because many of their supporters said that they did not understand the need for four orthodox parties. All four were in agreement that biblical law should be the basis of Israeli state law. Agudat Yisrael insisted that this be made compulsory; the other parties in the bloc were less extreme in their demands.

The Communists advocated Israel's joining the Soviet bloc as "the only guarantee of full independence," to quote Party Secretary Mikunis.

The splinter parties contesting the elections all complained about discrimination. Women were represented by the Wizo List, which called for a fair representation of women in parliament "to prevent the clerical parties from incorporating into the State code archaic religious laws which would prejudice the legal and social position of women."

Sephardi Jews claimed that they were not represented proportionally in the civil service, while the Yemenite Jews also felt that only parliamentary representation would protect their interests.

VOTING PATTERNS SINCE INDEPENDENCE
(1949-69)

An analysis[13] of the election results to the Knesset reveals that although the Israeli electorate tripled in size between the first and seventh elections this growth was not reflected in the results. Despite the often large initial differences in character between veteran (preindependence) Israelis and the newcomers, existing political frameworks effectively absorbed and channeled the new voters. The number of successful parties in the elections remained fairly stable, even as smaller, peripheral groups, representing factional or local interests, failed to capture the public eye.

The Labour movement (comprised of Mapai, Mapam, Ahdut, Haavoda, and Rafi) polled 47.7 percent of the vote in 1955, 51.4 in 1959, and 49.73 in 1969. Its leader has so far been Mapai, which has generally polled twice as much as any other labor party. The average for over 20 years of

TABLE 7

Contending Parties, First to Eighth Knesset

Knesset	Number of Contending Parties	Number of Successful Parties (over 1 percent of vote)
1	21	12
2	17	15
3	18	12
4	24	12
5	14	11
6	17	13
7	19	12
8	21	9

independence shows that labor has commanded about half the popular vote, a record of great stability.

Affiliated to Mapai are small Arab labor parties, polling about 4 percent of the vote. Mapai has never yet established a majority government and has always been dependent on coalition partners, both in and outside labor, who have in turn determined the moderate and national character of the government.

The Nationalist parties (Conservative, Nationalist, and Liberal) dropped as a group from 29 percent in the first three Knessets to 27.5 in 1961 and 1965, and 26.08 in 1969, a slow but perceptible decline. In 1949 the bloc was led by Herut, but in 1951 leadership passed to the General Zionists (later called Liberals). In 1955 Herut was again in the lead, the General Zionists dropping from 16.2 percent in 1951 to 10.2 in 1955 and 6.2 in 1959. For the 1969 elections Herut and the Liberals set up a parliamentary bloc named Gahal, but the joint list won only 21.67 percent of the vote. A faction that broke away from Herut, called the Free Centre, won 1.2 percent, while another small party, the Progressives--which did not follow the Liberals into Gahal--called itself the Independent Liberal Party and won 3.21 percent in 1969.

The Religious parties, comprising the various religious parties that have accepted parliamentary rule, have won an average of 12-15 percent of the vote. In the 1969 elections, the National Religious Party won 9.74 percent, Agudat Yisrael won 3.22, and its socialist religious wing, Poalei Agudat Yisrael, won 1.83.

70

At the extreme left, the pro-Soviet New Communist Party (Rakah) won 2.84 percent, the pro-Zionist Israel Communist Party won 1.15, and the "fellow-traveler" New Force List won 1.23.

Small parties rarely have overcome the 1 percent barrier. In 1949 the Israel Freedom Fighters (Lehi) and the Women's International Zionist Organization (Wizo) won a seat each. In 1951, communal interests were represented by a Yemenite and two Sephardis. David Ben Gurion won a seat in 1969 for a while heading his own State List, after breaking with Mapai, which he had led for several decades.

Average participation has been 83 percent of those entitled to vote. The massive immigration of the years 1949-51, as well as subsequent waves from various lands, changed the composition of the electorate.

In 1948, 65 percent of all Israelis had been born abroad. Of these, 85 percent were from Europe and the West and only 15 percent from Moslem countries. Immigration reduced the percentage of Israeli-born from 35 to 25 percent in 1951, but these rose again to 44 percent by 1968, when only 28.8 percent of the voters were Jews from Europe and 27.2 percent were Jews from Islamic countries of Asia and Africa.[14]

In 1968, 31.2 percent of the population lived in the three major cities of Jerusalem, Haifa, and Tel Aviv, 51 percent lived in small towns, and 18 percent in the rural areas. Of the Jewish population, 88.6 percent was urban and 11.4 rural. The famous <u>kibbutz</u> collective villages accounted for only 3.5 percent of the Jewish population; Israel's minority groups (Moslems, Christians, and Druzes) were divided fairly equally between towns (43.2 percent) and villages (56.8).

Voting patterns clearly were discernible in the <u>kib-butz</u> and <u>moshav</u> villages where large proportions of the electorate voted for whichever party their village was affiliated with, while the Arab vote generally has been shared between pro-Labour lists (45 percent), the New Communists (25-30 percent), and the balance divided by all other parties. In 1969 there were 406,200 Arab citizens out of a total population of 2,841,100. Arab residents of territories administered by the Israel Army since 1967 do not vote for the Knesset, as their citizenship (mainly Jordanian) has not been affected. The only exception has been the Old City of Jerusalem and its suburbs, formerly under Jordanian military occupation (1948-67), where all residents were granted--and also availed themselves of--the right to vote for the municipality and Histadrut branch of the reunited city. The Jerusalem municipal area is under civilian, not military, administration.

The urban vote, as will be seen by the above, is the most important part of the electorate. Between the 1965 and 1969 elections, the electorate increased by 17 percent, due mainly to the accretion of young people voting for the first time. Only 20 percent of the increase was due to immigration. The local government electorate increased by 23 percent, including the Old City of Jerusalem and suburbs.*

The distribution of votes to the Seventh Knesset by major blocs shows that, compared with previous elections, Labour suffered a slight drop of 1.9 percent while the Religious bloc gained 0.7 percent and the Centre rose by 1.0 percent. In the Jewish cities, Labour retained its power losing slightly to the Centre and Religious in rural areas. In all minority-inhabited areas, Labour lost support, declining from 21.6 to 14.3 percent, these votes going largely to the New Communists. Gahal won 81 percent of its support in the cities compared with 68 percent of the votes for Labour and 61 percent of those for the Religious parties. Rural voters supplied only 4 percent of Gahal votes but provided 15 percent of the Labour gains and 19 percent of the Religious vote. A high proportion of kibbutz members voted Labour, but they accounted for only 7 percent of its total votes. The New Communists won 77 percent of their support from Arab voters.

The voting patterns of different quarters in the major cities show that neighborhood voting blocs existed mainly in respect of the Religious parties, as evidenced by the heavy proreligious vote in certain quarters of Jerusalem

---

*Jerusalem was partitioned in 1948 along the battle lines of the War of Independence, the larger part (in area and population) known as the New City, retained by Israel, and the Old City, about one-fifth the total area, captured by the Arab Legion of Trans-Jordan. The Jewish inhabitants of the Old City were taken prisoner and later released to Israel; their homes were destroyed as were their Holy Places. Jordan declared her annexation of Jerusalem's Old City, an act never recognized by the United Nations. In 1967 Jordan launched an attack on the New City from the Old, but was defeated and expelled. Israel regards Jerusalem as her traditional capital and rejects the idea of its repartition. Holy sites of Christianity and Islam are protected by Israeli law and are supervised by the respective clergy of both faiths.

(Table 8). Labour won in all three cities, but in Tel Aviv
the Centre came a close second, reflecting the city's commercial interests. The same trends noted in the Knesset
elections also marked the local government elections, held
the same day, where these were still more pronounced. The
Labour parties lost about 6 percent, the Religious bloc
gained 0.6 percent, and the Centre grew by 4.1 percent. If
one makes a further distinction between municipalities and
local councils (rural areas), these trends are even more
pronounced. Thus, Labour lost 10 percent of its support in
local council elections compared with 3.7 in the municipalities. This indicates a weakening of Labour strength in
rural areas. In the three major cities, a comparison between the Knesset and local government election results indicates split-ticket voting. In Jerusalem, the capital,
Labour received 10.6 percent more votes in the local than
in the Knesset elections. This was explained by the personal popularity of the Labour candidate for mayor. In Tel
Aviv, the Centre won 6.8 percent more in the municipal elections than in the Knesset vote from the same city, for the
opposite reason. (This trend in Tel Aviv developed in 1973
into a Likud victory.)

TABLE 8

Average Vote Distribution to the Seventh Knesset,
by Percentages

Locality	Labour	Reli- gious	Centre	Commu- nist	Others (mainly Arab Lists)
Municipalities	46	11	<u>30</u>	1	12
Local councils	45	16	18	1	20
Veteran Jewish towns	48	14	<u>30</u>	3	5
Immigrant Jewish towns	<u>53</u>	14	27	3	5
Arab towns	5	5	2	<u>51</u>	57
Veteran Jewish vil- lages	<u>56</u>	16	24	3	1
Immigrant Jewish villages	42	<u>33</u>	19	1	5
Arab villages	15	<u>10</u>	3	<u>28</u>	44

Note: Underlined figures are especially significant
ones.

73

Labour showed strength among the veteran Jewish villages (kibbutzim largely) and the new towns inhabited largely by immigrants. The Religious parties were most successful in new Jewish villages, largely of the moshav type, inhabited by new immigrants. Many of these villages are populated by observant Jews from the Moslem countries. The Centre, representing commercial interests, not unexpectedly found its largest support in Israel's towns and cities, while the Communists (mainly Rakah) drew their strength from Israel's Arab towns and villages, which also voted heavily for the progovernment Arab labor lists. It is interesting to note that the procommunist vote was much stronger in Arab towns than in the villages, where agriculture is still carried on in a traditional economy and society.

THE PARTIES THAT FAILED

The Fourth Knesset elections in 1959 were contested by no less than 24 parties, of which the majority failed to obtain even 1 percent of the vote. Although politically of no consequence at all, they remain historically interesting (Table 9).

The proliferation of small and unsuccessful parties prior to elections indicates that while the public tends to support existing and stable lists many minor politicians feel each time that they had something new to offer, despite the discouraging evidence of the previous election. In 1965, for example, the following small parties failed to win any seats: the Yemenite Religious Party, the Union of Israeli Yemenites, the Central Arab List, the New Immigrant Party, and the Union of North Africans. By the time the 1969 elections were held, however, the number of minor parties contending and losing the elections was reduced to three: the Land of Israel List, the Peace List, and the Young Israel Party. The first new list to have overcome the 1 percent barrier successfully was Haolam Hazeh (New Force), which in 1969 polled 1.23 percent of the vote. As noted, the failure of immigrant and communal lists is perhaps the most important fact, showing that by and large immigrants have been quickly absorbed into existing political patterns. (See also Table A-3. Note that 11 parties failed in the 1973 elections.)

TABLE 9

The Parties That Failed in the Fourth Knesset

Party	Description	Votes Won
Progress and Labour	Arab family list	4,649
Third Force	Trotskyite	574
Independent Faction	Arab family list	3,813
North African Union	Immigrant group	7,915
Invalids and Victims of the Holocaust	War veterans	1,811
Yemenite Faction	Immigrant group	1,663
National Union of the Sepharadi and Oriental Communities	Immigrant group	2,393
National Sephardi Party and Oriental Communities	Immigrant group	3,145
Independent List of North Africans	Immigrant group	1,577
New Immigrant Party	Immigrant group	622
Bund Socialist Union	Left-wing anti-Zionist	1,309
Israel Arab Labour Party	Affiliated to Ahdut Haavoda	3,363

THE POLITICAL ACCULTURATION OF IMMIGRANTS

The mass immigration of Jews from Moslem countries to Israel changed the balance of the electorate during the first 10 years of independence but did not appreciably change the balance of power, which indicated a rapid acculturation to Israel's existing political establishment. In three sectors of political activity these immigrants quickly made their presence felt: in workers' committees, in the organizations of existing political parties, and in local government. The changes were felt from the bottom upward and principally in those areas that were largely settled by new immigrants. True, they do not yet hold a proportionally large representation at the national level, but this in due course is bound to take place. In many small towns and development areas, several public posts will be in the hands of a few politically active individuals. A political party worker who is a member of a local workers' committee may well be also a member of the local village, township, or regional council. This overlapping of roles facilitates the transfer of key positions at the local levels to members of the larger local communities.[15]

There are no official statistics regarding the communal affiliation of local council members. But data collected privately, by S. Weiss, on local councils up to 1965 indicate definite trends.

In 1950, only 13 percent of the members of Israel's local councils were Jewish immigrants from Moslem countries. By 1965, their proportion had risen to 44 percent and, in some development towns, 62 percent. These immigrants also rose in status within the councils of local government. In the early 1950s only 11 percent of the chairmen of local councils and mayors of municipalities were immigrants from Moslem countries. By the second half of the 1960s, they led 40 percent of all local councils and 60 percent of the development town municipalities.

In contrast, the three major cities, Jerusalem, Tel Aviv, and Haifa, have not yet shown in their town council membership that representation that would be proportionate to the communal picture. In 1971, Jews from Moslem countries constituted 16 percent of the municipal council of Haifa, 22 percent in Tel Aviv, and 32 percent in Jerusalem.

Immigrant politicians from Moslem countries are markedly younger than European Jewish politicians, and a higher proportion are second generation--born in Israel. Among chairmen of local councils in development towns, about 50 percent were aged 40 or less upon taking office, while this age group supplied only 14 percent of the mayors of large towns and cities following the last elections. In the three large cities, 50 percent of the non-European Jews on municipal councils were born in Israel, whereas among the European Jews, only 10 percent were born in the country.

The phenomenon of sons of an underprivileged immigrant group reaching high status through local politics is familiar to students of the United States. In Israel, Jewish immigrants from Moslem countries quickly adapted themselves to the democratic process in order to better their station. Living in large joint families, they found organization and public relations to be simplified and votes en masse guaranteed. Political growth did not depend on formal education, nor did it necessitate a rupture with strong family ties and background through real or imagined sophistication.

However, politicians of this type have been quick to realize that any further climb toward the top, in Israel's technological society of the future, will require formal educational attainments, and many of them are to be found entering Israel's universities.

The possibility of advancing in status through existing parties--and particularly through the largest one, the Labour Party--was the main reason for the fact that politicians of Jewish immigrant communities from Moslem lands did not set up separate communal frameworks for the furtherance of personal, communal, or group interests. Although from time to time communally based political groups may be seen in development towns, these actually are indications of rivalries between groups within communities, not of non-European Jews against Europeans.

The failure of communally based parties at the national level in seven Knesset elections is one of the most important indexes of the degree of acculturation of community and immigrant groups. The small communal parties of the 1950s were in fact vehicles of joint family interests, and they dwindled as their prospective voters showed their preferences for the larger and better-established noncommunal parties. The record of 20 years shows that any political force seeking to win strength in the opposition by playing up communal discord in Israel is bound to fail. Although both Herut on the right and the Communists on the left may have had such ideas, they do not seem to have impressed the electorate.

The sociologist H. Smith in his analysis of voting patterns remarks that the Labour Party was best able to retain its popularity among immigrants from Moslem countries in two instances: in development towns where there was a fair degree of homogeneity between the population and local politicians--that is, that they were all largely of the same communal background--and in those places where no community had a clear majority but where all were mixed together. The problematic areas, from a sociological as well as a political point of view, tend to be those where communal or income differentials are visible. An indication of this has been the drop in support for the Labour Party among the poorer inhabitants of the three main cities, balanced by a stronger vote for the ruling party in the wealthier parts of town.

Naturally, all parties are competing for this large potential vote, and this offers a chance to young, dynamic, and public-spirited figures of immigrant communities to strive for success within the existing political framework.

Were they not given the chance to express themselves in such a democratic manner it is highly probable that they would have sought an independent political form of expression.

A major factor leading to this development was the "gentlemen's agreement" of the major Zionist parties during the 1950s, when they divided among themselves the areas of political activity among the newcomers. This arrangement, together with the settlement of many newcomers in brand new towns and villages founded for the purpose of giving them homes, jobs, and futures, quickly turned the influx of refugees from Moslem lands into a citizen population cognizant of its rights and duties within the political democracy of Israel--and immediately so at the local government level.

Immigrant politicians definitely are on their way up in local government, in Histadrut workers' committees, and in political party hierarchies, thus guaranteeing an ever-growing representation for the legitimate demands of their communities within the existing framework. That the major demand to be heard today is for better educational facilities for the younger generation, in the hope that these will strengthen them as responsible citizens of the future, is most encouraging.[16]

THE ORGANIZED ELECTORATE: POLITICAL
YOUTH MOVEMENTS AND VILLAGES

Almost all political parties in Israel have established youth movements[17] designed to attract teen-agers with a program that combines scouting, the outdoor life, pioneer idealism, patriotism, and cultural events. There were 134,000 youngsters organized in these movements in 1967, a third of all Israelis between the ages of 11 and 18. Almost all movements are open to boys and girls equally. They supply their parent political parties with a steady flow of suitably trained cadres for leadership, as well as ensuring, by the fostering of a comradely spirit, the future allegiance of movement graduates to the party ideology. At the age of 18 many movement graduates join the army en bloc as part of the Nahal military farming units, which combine military with agricultural training centered in kibbutz villages and from which many young men and women go on to settle in these villages after their regular military service. The movements have been of prime importance in the integration of immigrant youth in the Israeli way of life.

The principal youth movements are the following:

1. The organization of Working and School Youth, founded in 1925, with about 99,000 members in 1967. The organization is affiliated to the Histadrut and is connected with Mapai. (Hanoar Haoved Vehalomed)

2. The Israel Boy and Girl Scout Federation, officially nonpolitical, is under direct government patronage. It has 15,000 members. (Hatsofim)

3. The Young Guards Association is strongly socialist and kibbutz-oriented. It has a membership of 7,500 and is affiliated to Mapam. (Hashomer Hatsair)

4. The Immigrant Camps Movement, affiliated to Ahdut Haavoda. (Mahanot Ha-Olim)

5. The Sons of Akiva, affiliated to the Hapoel Hamizrahi Party, stresses religion. Its membership is 20,000. (Bnei Akiva)

6. Ezra, also religious, belongs to the Poalei Agudat Yisrael Party and has 3,300 members.

7. Beitar belongs to the Herut Party and has 5,000 members.

8. The Young Maccabees, with 6,000 members, is affiliated to the Liberal Party. (Maccabi Hatsair)

9. The Religious Working Youth Association, affiliated to Hapoel Hamizrahi, has 5,000 members. (Hanoar Haoved Hadati)

10. The Communist Youth League, affiliated to Maki, no figures available. (Banki)

As noted, Israeli villages also are organized largely on political lines. The majority of collectives (kibbutz villages) belong to the following bodies:

1. The National Kibbutz Movement, affiliated to Mapan and the Young Guards. Founded in 1927, it now includes 74 kibbutz villages with a population of 31,000. (Kibbutz Artzi)

2. The United Kibbutz Movement, founded in 1927. Including 58 villages with a total population of 25,300, it is associated through Ahdut Haavoda with the Israel Labour Party. (Hakibbutz Hameuhad)

3. (a) The Union of Kibbutz Villages, founded in 1951, has 85 villages and 30,500 people. Most of its members are associated with the Israel Labour Party. Also included in its framework are 6 kibbutzim, 20 moshavim, and 5 youth villages that belong to the Independent Liberal movement. (Ichud Hakibbutzim) (b) The Zionist Youth. (Hanoar Hatsioni)

4. The Religious Kibbutz Movement, founded in 1930, has 13 villages and 4,000 souls, affiliated to Hapoel Hamizrahi. (Hakibbutz Hadati)

Most of the moshav (cooperative) villages are organized into the following:

1. The Moshav Movement, 220 villages, population 85,000, pro-Labour.
2. Union of Religious Cooperative Villages, 62 villages with 25,000 people, affiliated to Hapoel Hamizrahi.
3. Farmers' Union, 54 villages with 15,000. Tends toward the center bloc.
4. The Zionist Workers, with 18 villages, 5,400 souls, connected with the Independent Liberals.
5. Cooperative Agricultural Centre, connected to Herut and Beitar, 13 villages, 3,000 souls.
6. Religious Villages, affiliated to Poalei Agudat Yisrael, 9 villages with 3,000 people.

Apart from the Histadrut, which encompasses 58 percent of the adult population of Israel, there are three other major trade union bodies:

1. Hapoel Hamizrahi, founded 1922, organizes religious workers, with 100,000 members.
2. The National Labour Federation, founded in 1934 by the Revisionists, is today affiliated to the Herut Party and has 80,000 members. It maintains a workers' health insurance fund like the Kupat Holim of the Histadrut.
3. Poalei Agudat Yisrael has a membership of 27,000 orthodox workers.

THE KIBBUTZ IN ISRAELI POLITICS

The early Zionist pioneers who came to redeem themselves, their land, and their society established communal and cooperative villages enjoying internal autonomy and autarchy in which they evolved a unique way of life, which they saw as the implementation of socialist Zionism. Their dedication produced a nationalist patriotism in which every rock and hill of the Land of Israel was imbued with biblical association and meaning, in which village life itself was idealized and the city spurned. The kibbutz member was accorded a high place in national prestige, and Jewish urban youth was encouraged to join kibbutz villages via the youth movement channels. In Jewish communities abroad, parallel youth movements oriented to a _kibbutz_ ideology, also developed and induced many thousands of young immigrants to come specifically in order to join a _kibbutz_. In coordination with the Jewish Agency and the Histadrut, _kibbutz_ villages were set up in desolate areas of Mandatory Palestine, establishing agricultural and political facts. When war broke out in 1948, this policy showed its value: land defended by _kibbutz_ villages was almost entirely retained by Israel. Empty territories were overrun by the Arabs. Kibbutz villages have provided Israeli politics with much of its leadership: the late Eshkol was a member of Kibbutz Degania, his successor, Golda Meir belonged to Kibbutz Merhavia, and her deputy, Alon, comes from Kibbutz Ginossar. The _kibbutz_ also has given the Israeli army some of its best officers and jet fighter pilots. It is therefore something of a surprise to note that only 3.5 percent of Israel's people live on a _kibbutz_. The unique discipline expected of a member in a thoroughly communal society may perhaps be too much for the rather individualistic Jew coming from a long tradition of independent urban living. (Compare the idealization in India, and abroad, of the _ashram_ with the actual number of people who live in such institutions.) It has been pointed out[18] that a third of all the _kibbutzim_ and most of the _moshavim_ are connected with Mapai, in which a strong agrarian lobby is reflected. Whereas before independence the agrarian lobby was paramount, since then the growing urbanization of Israel has reduced its influence; this decline will probably continue.

VOTING PATTERNS OF ISRAELI
MINORITY GROUPS

Israel's minority is largely Palestinian Arab by culture and language, but divided by religion into Christians of various denominations, Moslems, and Druzes. Not all Arabs vote for recognizably Arab lists, rendering statistics rather approximate than accurate. The fact that a high percentage of these former Palestinian Arabs participate actively in Israeli politics is an indication of their integration, but this integration itself has two forms: one is traditional, in which the Arab minority links itself to various Jewish political elements and is connected with government; the other is that of protest, by supporting those opposition elements who appear to be supporting Arab nationalism. Yet, the protest itself is conducted largely in a democratic manner.

The 1948 War was a traumatic experience for the Israelis, who won, and even more so for the Arabs, who lost.
Those Palestinian Arabs who refused to join the refugee
exodus became Israeli citizens; but their leadership had
been the first to leave. With this breakdown of traditional
society, adaptation to the Western-type democracy of Israel
was less problematical for Israel's Arab citizens, especially for the younger men and women among them. In 1966
about 50 percent of Israel's Arabs had been born after
1948, while another 25 percent had been under 14 in that
year. This meant that only 25 percent could remember the
days of the British Mandate. In economic terms, the Israeli
Arabs enjoy high standards of living. The contrast between
the Arabs who stayed and enjoyed the benefits of Israeli
government and the Arabs who left to a most uncertain fate
as refugees is evident. Israeli Arabs have shown an active
interest in the Knesset and local elections, with an average participation of 88 percent in elections. In 1969,
Arabs voted in the following percentages: Mapai, 12.6;
Mapam, 9.2; Herut, 1.9; national religious, 4.5; Progressives, 1.1; Communists, 23.1; prolabor Arab lists, 42.7;
others, 5.1. Yet, by no stretch of their imagination could
they accept Zionist principles, nor have they been asked
to do so. They established political "parties" representing
clan interests, allied pragmatically to those Jewish political forces that they felt would protect their interests
in exchange for votes. That no single Arab party ever captured the votes of the entire minority population is due
perhaps to the fissiparous tendencies of Arab politics, a
feature to be seen elsewhere in the Middle East. The multiplicity of clan-based parties enabled Arab chieftains to
participate simultaneously in traditional feudal, as well
as democratic, political structures, and voting has tended
to reflect clan loyalties. Thus, some Arab "parties" allied themselves with the ruling labor bloc*; for tactical
advantage they sometimes forged alliances with the religious parties and even with the nationalist Herut. Opposition of a more strident sort found its expression in the
Arab vote for the Communist Party, particularly the Rakah
wing, which quite openly supported Egyptian policies and
is a faithful echo of Soviet ideas and arguments. The
granting of legality to such sentiments in the context of

---

*In the Sixth Knesset, four Arab members represented
the lists of Cooperation and Unity, and Agriculture and
Development, both affiliated to Mapai.

the Israel—Arab confrontation may at first sight be a little surprising, but it has proved to have been a necessary safety valve.

NOTES

1. M. Louvish, How Israel's Democracy Works (Jerusalem: Jewish Agency, 1970). See also E. Katz, "Platforms and Windows: Broadcasting's Role in Election Campaigns," International Communications Issue of Journalism Quarterly, Summer 1971, pp. 304–305.

2. Y. Freudenheim, Government in Israel (New York: Oceana Publications, 1967), p. 123. This is an excellent technical survey.

3. In the first five British elections since World War II, the number of the electorate turning out to vote has been as follows:

	1945 (73% voting)	1950 (84% voting)	1951 (82.6% voting)	1955 (76.8% voting)	1959 (78.7% voting)
Main Parties' Share of Votes:					
Conservative	9,960,809 30.3%	12,501,983 41.7%	13,724,418 47.98%	13,336,182 49.8%	13,734,336 49.3%
Labour	11,992,292 36.5%	13,295,736 46.4%	13,948,365 48.77%	12,405,130 46.3%	12,208,810 43.9%
Liberal	2,245,319 6.8%	2,621,489 9.1%	730,551 2.55%	722,400 2.7%	1,636,292 5.9%
Swing to Conservative	--	3.13%	1.1%	1.8%	1.5%
Seats These Votes Brought:					
Conservative	213	296	321	345	365
Labour	393	315	295	277	256
Liberal	12	9	6	6	6

Source: D. E. Butler, Electoral System in Britain 1918–1951) (Oxford: Oxford University Press, 1953).

4. G. Kraft, "Elections to the 7th Knesset and Local Authorities," Results of Elections (Jerusalem: Central Bureau of Statistics, 1970).

5. Knesset Elections Law, Sections 4, 57, 60; also A. Witkon, "Elections in Israel," Israel Law Review 5, no. 1 (January 1970).

6. Jerusalem Post, November 19, 1972; March 13, 1973.

7. Ibid., March 15, 1973.

8. Ibid., July 12, 1973.

9. Ibid., December 20, 1972.

10. Ibid., January 5, 1973.

11. Ibid., February 1, 1973.

12. M. Brilliant, "Policies, Parties, Men Seek Votes for First Assembly," Palestine Post, December 10, 1948.

13. H. Smith, Sixth Knesset Elections (Jerusalem: Hebrew University, 1967).

14. Data as released by the Central Bureau of Statistics, Jerusalem.

15. E. Salpeter, "Politics Break the Barrier," Ha'aretz (daily), June 9, 1971 (Hebrew).

16. Shevach Weiss, "Haherkev Ha-adati shel Hamanhigut Bamosadot Hamamlachtiim Vehamekomiim" ("The Ethnic Composition of Leadership in State and Local Government Institutions"), MOLAD (bimonthly) 28, no. 238 (April 1973): 357-366.

17. H. Barzel, Youth in Israel (Jerusalem: Jewish Agency, 1967).

18. Based on A. Etzioni, "Agrarianism in Israel's Party System," The Canadian Journal of Economics and Political Science 23, no. 3 (August 1957): 363-375.

CANDIDATE SELECTION

The Knesset, which literally means "congregation," is located in Jerusalem in a large, square building on a hilltop in the center of the city. It is Israel's sovereign parliament, unicameral, with 120 members.

These members attain their positions through elections for the parties to which they belong, and it is the assignment of a "real" place on the party list that determines a candidate's chance of actually reaching the Knesset more than any other single factor.[1] As in most countries practicing proportional representation, there is a fair measure of stability in the partisan composition of Israel's parliament. The candidates placed in "secure" positions at the top of their lists have a very high degree of expectation to be elected. The candidates placed on the lower, less fortunate part of the list are left with only negligible chances to enter the Knesset, and only holders of the intermediate "marginal" positions are really dependent on the changing moods of the electorate. The phenomenon corresponds, mutatis mutandis, to the placing of a candidate under the single constituency system into a "safe," as against a "doubtful" or "hopeless," constituency.

As in other "democracies," heightened significance attaches to the candidate-selection stage and to the bodies that formally nominate the candidates or materially influence their selection. The electoral law entrusts the nomination of candidates, in the case of preexisting Knesset parties, to the parties themselves. There is nothing in Israel resembling the U.S. primary, although this has been put forward in Labour Party circles.

The selection is made by a body or bodies authorized to do so by the respective party's bylaws. The Knesset representatives of the party do not ex officio take any decisive part in these proceedings except insofar as individual members participate in the bodies in question. In most cases the bylaws are none too explicit on the process of selection, and the matter is regulated on the theory that whatever decisions need to be taken in party affairs are left to a lower echelon in the party hierarchy, unless the higher echelon has chosen to take them itself or has expressly delegated them to a specific agency. The usual echelons are, in descending order: conference, council, central committee, political committee, secretariat. The nomenclature varies, and additional intermediate organs also are encountered. As might be expected, the real influence within this chain of bodies is in inverse order to their formal, hierarchical relationship, each smaller and ostensibly less authoritative body representing a greater concentration of leading personalities; and, although a reversal of the decisions of the smaller by the larger body is by no means uncommon, it is still the exception rather than the rule. The usual course is for the group of leaders in the smaller body to initiate the decision and to have it prevail in the final analysis. Reversals, when they do occur, signify that opinion within the leadership group is sharply divided.

In selecting a list of candidates, another consideration lends added weight to the smaller group: This operation involves many clashes of personal ambitions as well as of sectional or interest-group interests. Their satisfactory resolution by a large body sitting under the glare of publicity is well nigh impossible. The operation requires fine adjustments and give-and-take tactics. The tendency, therefore, is to leave the actual determination of the list to the smallest available formal group. Indeed, quite often even this proves to be unwieldy, and the composition of the list is entrusted to a specially selected ad hoc subcommittee of leaders or is decided by a few leaders who do not sit at all in a formal capacity but, because of their standing and prestige, are in a position to settle the thorny questions involved. Officially, of course, their work is regarded as a mere "recommendation" subject to approval by one of the larger formal party agencies.

The technique here described was modified in a few large parties as a result of the discontent manifested by the local branches at the undue influence of party leaders and workers entrenched in central party bodies. Occupa-

tional, economic, ideological, and regional interests may
conflict within a party, as well as the natural division
of young versus old. The latter factor is an acutely felt
one in Israel. Whereas the republic is young, its political leadership is old in years, and the process of infusing
new blood into politics is rather slow. To some extent,
Israel is a "gerontocracy."

A high proportion of Israel's politicians, of the
"old guard," are from Eastern Europe and Russia. Approximately 60 percent of the members of the Knesset to date
have come from these countries. About 25 percent are
Israeli-born, and their proportion, naturally, is rising.
Table 10 gives the geographical origins of Knesset members.
Of the Fourth Knesset members, 49 were university graduates,
21 had studied at university without completing their studies, 10 were trained in rabbinical studies, 22 had completed
a secondary education, 14 had not finished high school, and
4 had only an elementary education.

From the official biographies of members of the First
Knesset, one may sketch the following composite portraits.

The typical Mapai member was born about 1890 in Russia. As a secondary school student he was caught up in
Russian revolutionary affairs and Zionist matters, eventually immigrating to Israel (then Palestine) either imme-

TABLE 10

Geographical Origin of Knesset Members

Region of Birth	First Knesset	Second Knesset	Third Knesset	Fourth Knesset
Israel	13	20	18	23
Eastern Europe and Russia	86	84	83	77
Central Europe, includ- ing Germany	10	10	11	9
Balkans	1	1	2	1
Moslem countries	2	3	5	9
Western Europe	1	--	--	--
United States and Brit- ish Commonwealth	2	1	1	1
Other	5	1	--	--

Source: B. Akzin, "The Knesset," International Social Science Journal 13, no. 4 (1961): 571, Table 3.

diately after graduating from secondary school or in the middle of college. In Israel he probably worked for a few years as a manual farm laborer, but trade unionism eventually brought him into almost full-time political activity. The average Mapai member had been jailed by Russian, Turkish, or British police for his ideas. All Mapai members also were affiliated to the Histadrut. Several had trained as lawyers, and among the Mapai several members were prominent women leaders.

In contrast, the typical Mapam member was a great deal younger, having been born about 1910. Many Mapam members came from Poland and were trained as lawyers. Strongly ideological, the typical Mapam member was a founding member of a kibbutz and active in trade unionism.

The average religious member was born about 1905 in Rumania or Poland and usually had a religious training as a rabbi.

The typical Herut member was born about 1910, probably in Israel. Strongly nationalist, he was usually a poet, writer, or journalist. Invariably he had been arrested, or sought, by the British police.

On the Liberal (General Zionist) benches one found university-educated intellectuals and professionals, born about 1910, including both native Israelis and immigrants. Business interests were strongly represented.

Progressive (Independent Liberal) members usually were German-born, about 1910, highly educated professionals and intellectuals.

The Sephardi members of the Knesset were born about 1890 in Jerusalem or Tiberias, of ancient Jewish families. Many had been civil servants under the Ottoman Empire, or were editors.

Only two members of the First Knesset had had any parliamentary experience outside Israel, and these had been in the Polish Sejm.

Although women constituted about half the voting population, female representation in the Knesset has been rather low. In 1969, only 7 women faced 113 men in the Knesset. (Nevertheless, Golda Meir may be said to have qualitatively redressed this balance, like Indira Gandhi and Sirimavo Bandaranaike.

Only once, in 1949, did a nonparty women's organization (Wizo) contest, and win, a seat. Thereafter, the Wizo women withdrew from politics and have concentrated on social welfare instead.

In the 1969 elections, the average age of members was 55 years, the oldest 82. Half gave their addresses in the

big cities, the other half in towns and villages. Their
declared occupations were: farmers, 22; rabbis, 3; lawyers,
21; engineers, 2; officials, 18; professors, 2; teachers,
14; economists, 2; journalists, 13; and executives (commercial), 4. Five said that their occupation was "member of
the Knesset," and four said they were "ministers" by profession. The remaining ten members represented each one
of the following professions: linguist, weaver, spinner,
sociologist, cooperative member, social worker, local council chairman, travel agent, headmaster, and unemployed.
The number of members whose real vocation is "politician"
is probably larger than indicated by these statements.

Changes in the membership of the Seventh Knesset were
as follows: Out of the 120 members, only 32 were really
new faces, but they were younger men on the average than
the men they replaced.

	Under 40	40 to 60	Over 60	Average Age
New members	10	25	4	48.6
Outgoing members	1	19	19	56.4

Nevertheless, the average age of the members of the Seventh
Knesset as a whole was 54.5 years. Of the new members,
seven were native-born Israelis, three came from Asia and
Africa, six were professionals, two were farmers, and only
two were professional politicians. Notably absent among
the new members are people with experience in the army,
diplomacy, economics, medicine, engineering, or social work
--all fields that are often the subject of Knesset debates.[2]

One gains the impression that Israeli parliamentarians
are bound by party discipline more than their U.S. counterparts, for example. A discrete way of expressing dissent
is for a member to absent himself from voting, if he dis-
agrees with his whip. Members are expected to clear their
positions with their party before voting or presenting private members' bills. Members of coalition parties are
bound by strict rules and may not oppose coalition policy.

Debates are held specifically on party lines when the
subject matter is:

the formation or dismissal of the cabinet
the budget
foreign affairs
defense
motions of no-confidence

If the Knesset Committee rules that a given debate is to be
held on party lines, time is allotted for speeches by party
in order of size, with a minimum of 10 minutes per party.
The opposition generally opens, followed by the government.

THE PARLIAMENTARY PARTY (SI'AH)

The si'ah (plural: si'ot) is a major component of the
Assembly and forms the link between the political parties
of Israel and the sovereign legislature. It hears reports
from party ministers, studies policy, and guides members
in speech making and voting. The si'ah may propose a vote
of no-confidence in the government, whereas an individual
member only may put a question to a minister on a point of
policy or execution of policy. Members wishing to table
motions for the agenda in the plenum require the prior consent of the si'ah they belong to. Time is allocated by the
speaker to the si'ah, and not to individual members. In
debates on party lines, the speakers represent not necessarily their own private opinions but the ideas of the
si'ah as a whole. This may be contrasted with the British
system, where the member, though in fact speaking for his
party, is nominally at least regarded as speaking for his
constituency.
The si'ah also decides on its representatives to the
various Knesset committees. Some committees are held in
higher prestige than others, and members seated on them
are regarded with correspondingly different degrees of importance.
In 1972-73, the major committees were the Finance Committee, chaired by Israel Kargman of the Labour Alignment
(formerly chairman of the Labour si'ah and of the Coalition
Executive), and the Foreign Affairs and Security Committee,
headed by Hayim Tsadok, also of Labour, and formerly minister of Commerce and Industry.
While party discipline is expected of si'ah members,
the main feature of division in nearly all si'ot is the disparity of age between the si'ah leaders, who average 60
years, and the "young Turks," who average 40. The si'ah
of the Labour Alignment is subject to decisions taken at
party headquarters in all matters affecting the party ideology; and to ensure coordination, the present chairman of
the Labour si'ah, Moshe Bar'am, takes part in all meetings
of the Labour Party Executive. Sometimes decisions are
taken jointly by the executive of the party and its si'ah,
especially when they might have bearing on the stability

90

of the coalition--which at present includes the Religious Party and the Independent Liberals. In major political debates, such as that preceding the decision to return to the Jarring talks, the prime minister and other Labour ministers take part in si'ah deliberations. The Executive of the Labour si'ah also participates in the Alignment Bureau, a limited Labour forum. The Executive is composed of 16 members: 9 Mapai, 2 Rafi, 2 Ahdut Haavoda, and 3 Mapam. Two Labour ministers are delegated the responsibility of maintaining constant contact between the cabinet and the Labour si'ah. They are Ministers Galili and Shapira. The Coalition Executive (1973) is composed of 16 members: 11 Labour, 3 National Religious Party (Mafdal), 1 Independent Liberal, and 1 Arab.

Some ministers will appear at si'ah consultations only when they concern their ministries. Others will appear regardless of topic. The si'ah also may initiate debates and on occasion may even oppose government proposals for the agenda, as when the Labour si'ah defeated a government proposal to raise the cost of television licenses.

Dissent within the si'ah occurs in other parties, too. One accepted method of dissent is for a member to absent himself during a debate. However, dissenters are rarely censured, although the Labour Party has been known to send written reprimands to "undisciplined" members. It is extremely rare for members to "cross the floor" from one si'ah to another, although this has happened once or twice in the history of the Knesset. Small si'ot generally do not suffer from internal dissent, although the breakup of the two-man Haolam Hazeh faction into two, warring, one-man factions may prove the exception to the rule. Party discipline is generally laxer when the matter at stake is not regarded as fundamental, as when religious members may differ regarding a problem that all agree is completely secular.

The Gahal bloc includes 14 Herut and 12 Liberal members, led by an eight-man Executive that tends to exhibit more independence vis-à-vis its parent parties than, for example, the Labour bloc. The Gahal si'ah, for example, selected its ministers to the cabinet while it was in the coalition, and not the party centers, which had to ratify its choice. In the Gahal si'ah, whip discipline is less often used than in the Labour or religious si'ot, and members often are allowed to vote according to their own conscience. When, for example, the Israel pound was devalued in 1968, Gahal ministers supported the move over the objections of the Gahal parliamentary si'ah.

Communist si'ah members apparently have little scope for originality and toe the party line most faithfully.[3]

THE POWER OF THE KNESSET
MEMBER (QUESTIONS)

Israel has accepted the principle of the executive being responsible to the legislature (Knesset). One of the main ways in which this control is exercised is through the question (sheilta) put to ministers by members.[4] In theory the members are to report to parliament on the deeds or misdeeds of ministers, and so constant supervision is to be ensured. In a study made in Jerusalem, 8,000 questions submitted during the tenure of the Sixth Knesset were examined. One-third of all questions were submitted by only three members of the Knesset, Uri Avneri (New Force List), Yosef Tamir (Free Centre), and Shmuel Mikunis (Maki). The total number was a record for all Knessets, yet most members of the Sixth Knesset who were neither ministers nor deputy ministers refrained from asking questions. Among abstainers were such prominent members as Ben Gurion, Begin, Meir, and Rosen.

Plotting the frequency of questions on a graph model of the party distribution, with the vertical axis going from extreme secularists to extreme religious politicians, and the horizontal axis going from extreme left to extreme right, the results indicated a preponderance of questions put to the House by extreme political groups. The identification of the parliamentary role of questions with extreme opposition groups has tended, according to the thesis, to reduce the value and importance of the question itself as a parliamentary device for control of the government.

Ministers questioned most often are those in charge of Defense, Foreign Affairs, Transport, Finance, Labour, and Education, in that order. The prime minister was called upon to answer only 4 percent of all questions.

Members were impelled to ask questions by their personal interest, their ideological bent, the importance they attached to the subject and respondent, and by the degree of criticism that the question afforded. Members tried to ask questions that they felt would interest the public. Members rarely put questions during recess; and questions dropped off by 90 percent during the Six Day War, when presumably members were otherwise preoccupied.

Only 13 percent of members availed themselves of the
right to put a supplementary question. This apparently
was related to the physical presence of members in the
chamber. Uri Avneri, member for the New Force, held two
records: he put the largest number of questions for any
individual member as well as the largest number of supple-
mentaries. Although ministers are supposed to reply within
21 days, the speaker has never gone on record as stating
that a minister has failed to reply. An average question
is in fact replied to only after 54 days. Several questions
were replied to immediately, but 150 received replies only
after more than 200 days. Several questions had to wait
for over a year for a reply to be given.

The minister fastest to reply has been the minister
of Finance, averaging 32 days; the slowest, the prime minister, with 105 days. Some ministers will hasten to reply
to political opponents but will be tardy in answering members of their own party. Others do the opposite, and again
some are quite impartial in their delay. Speed in reply is
connected to the image the respondent has of himself within
his party, and of the image of his party. Speed in reply
also depends on the importance attributed by the respondent
to the questioner and the subject matter. Information
gleaned from the press was the basis of 44 percent of the
questions. Extreme politicians tended to quote the press
more than moderate ones. An analysis of newspapers cited
shows a low proportion of papers belonging to parties.
Sources most often cited were Haaretz (independent daily),
35 percent; Maariv, 20 percent; Yediot, 9 percent; Davar,
7 percent; Israel Radio, 5 percent; and foreign press, 4
percent. It is interesting to note that members generally
do not quote their own party papers.

The findings are summarized in noting that question
time in the Knesset is a largely ineffectual exercise. Out
of 80 cases, in 35 percent of the questions, ministers
were not asked to do anything. Only in 20 percent of the
questions where action was urged was any action in fact
taken. In 12 percent of the questions where ministers actually did something, it was demonstrated that there was
no causality between the question and the action. It appears then that questions are put to the House by the opposition to demonstrate that it exists, or by coalition back-
benchers who wish to make themselves heard. It is noted
that the speaker of the seventh Knesset has advocated reform of question procedures.

NOTES

1. E. S. Likhovski, <u>Israel's Parliament--The Law of the Knesset</u> (Oxford: Clarendon, 1971).

2. A. Brichte, "Membership Changes in the Seventh Knesset," <u>State and Government</u> 1, no. 2 (1971) (Hebrew).

3. Ibid., pp. 70-72.

4. Based on A. Diskin, "Trends and Questions in the House (Sixth Knesset)," M.A. Thesis, Hebrew University, 1971.

**GOVERNMENT BY
COALITION**

MAIN POLITICAL ISSUES

The rules governing Israel's coalition governments originally began as types of "gentlemen's agreements," but the exigencies of politics eventually compelled them to be put into writing, first as "Basic Principles of the Cabinet," presented to the Knesset for approval together with a request for a vote of confidence and, ultimately, as a Basic Law of constitutional character defining the rights and duties of the government (1968).

An important element has been the rule of collective responsibility. In 1959, it was stated in the government program that "collective responsibility applies to all members of the Cabinet and to all the parties participating in the Government. The basic principles and decisions of the cabinet are obligatory on all members of the cabinet and their parties." Abstention from voting in the Knesset on the cabinet's decisions was permissible only with the cabinet's approval or after resignation from the cabinet before the vote. A vote against cabinet policy, or even abstention, was regarded as equivalent to resignation from the cabinet.

The 1968 Basic Law (the Government) defined the government as the executive authority of the state and placed its seat in Jerusalem. (The cabinet, as distinct from the Knesset, occasionally held its meetings in Tel Aviv, as well as in Jerusalem.) The prime minister had to be a member of the Knesset, a rule that did not necessarily apply to the other ministers.

The following pages discuss some of the main issues that have preoccupied Israel's governments and have determined the fate of its coalitions.

A U.S. observer of Israeli politics,[1] in surveying the
political transitions since independence, notes Prime Minister Ben Gurion's resignation in June 1963 as the end of an
era. Indeed, Ben Gurion's break with Mapai, his founding
of the Rafi Party, and later, when Rafi returned to the fold
of the Labour Party, his insistence on retaining independence of action as leader of a small national list: all
marked the last phases of an impressive personal career--a
career that, beginning in the 1920s, had assumed leadership
of the labor wing of Zionism in the 1930s and declared Israel's independence in 1948.

The internal strains of the Lavon Affair, which at the
time shook the very foundations of the Labour parties, have
been largely overcome, notwithstanding the shock created
by Ben Gurion's departure. Barring a slight dip at the
polls, Labour sustained its strength, and largely due to
the efforts of the late Prime Minister Eshkol and Golda
Meir, unity has been maintained. Yet, the Labour-led coalition has faced and has overcome many more crises originating outside the Labour movement itself. Some related to
education, or the question of "who is a Jew." Only a
minority of the issues were drawn from foreign affairs,
the most notable being relations with postwar Germany and
the aftermath of the 1953, 1967, and 1973 wars with Egypt
and the other Arab states.

The first political crisis in the coalition, in 1948,
arose from the dispute between Labour and Centre regarding
the future of their paramilitary units, which could not
coexist in a democracy with the national army. The units
were dissolved and their men absorbed in the army, but 20
years later, campaign veterans are still arguing about
that crucial period in which Israel took a decisive step
for democracy. The question of education was a bone of
contention for many years between religious and secular
parties. As noted in Chapter 4, a compromise solution was
reached, establishing both secular and religious state
schools. Another question troubling many Israelis was the
moral propriety of accepting financial compensation from
Germany for the loss of 6 million Jews and their property
during the Nazi period. The compensation was paid by West
Germany, as East Germany refused to consider the question
of responsibility for Nazi war crimes. Herut (supported
here by the extreme left) was the main campaigner against
accepting the money, but the opposition failed to persuade
the government to change its mind. An agreement on repara-
tions was signed between West Germany and Israel, leading
eventually to full diplomatic relations between the two

countries. (East Germany rejected the idea of any relations with Israel.)[2]

In 1953, following the Stalinist anti-Jewish campaign in Russia, the General Zionists won the support of Ben Gurion, against the majority of Labour votes, to abolish the singing of the "Internationale" and the display of the Red Flag at Israeli Labour schools on May 1, as had been the custom since the days of Lenin. Only the Israeli flag and anthem were to be permitted.

From the time the first elected four-party coalition government of 12 members was approved by the Knesset on March 10, 1949 up to 1957, Ben Gurion had resigned the office of prime minister on four occasions and Sharett on two.[3] Cabinets had been reshuffled often because of political crises, deaths, differences in policy, or reasons of health. The longest period of cabinet stability was from June 1956 to February 1957, a total of eight months (during which there was a war with Egypt) and from October 1951 to May 1952, when the coalition consisted of Mapai and the religious bloc. A slightly longer period of relative calm extended from March 1949 to January 1950, although it was broken by threats from the religious bloc to resign. These threats came to a head in February 1950 over the issue of religious education for immigrant children. Then the nation's first threatened crisis took the form of a boycott of cabinet meetings by the three religious ministers. On a warning from the prime minister that nonattendance meant resignation, they returned; but, on June 22, 1950, the minister for Religious Affairs walked out, and the prime minister was compelled to resign on October 15, 1950 after attempts at conciliation had failed. Although the cabinet was reformed, it failed to work smoothly, and elections for the Second Knesset were held on July 30, 1951.

A new Mapai-Religious cabinet was sworn in on October 9, 1951, and in December 1952 it was enlarged by co-opting the General Zionists. Hapoel Hamizrahi, which until then had been in the opposition, also decided to join, giving the cabinet 87 votes in the House. In 1953 Ben Gurion resigned, for health reasons, being succeeded by Moshe Sharett. In August, the General Zionists walked out after Mapai suggested raising the minimal representation of parties to those winning at least 4 percent of the vote. Following Lavon's resignation as minister of Defense in 1955, Ben Gurion returned. However, Sharett as prime minister had a majority of only five, and new elections were held on July 26. Ben Gurion was again the prime minister, leading a coalition of five parties, including, for the first

time, Ahdut Ha'avoda and Mapam. The Progressive Party was
a member of nearly all the coalition governments. In the
midst of the major international crisis that led to the
Six Day War of 1967, a national unity coalition under Levi
Eshkol was created due to the entry of Herut and the General Zionists (Gahal bloc) into the cabinet. General Moshe
Dayan, representing Rafi, took over as minister of Defense,
and Menachem Begin and Yosef Sapir became ministers without
portfolio. Sapir and Dayan had held cabinet posts before,
but the unity displayed by Ben Gurion and Begin, in the
face of Egypt, was a remarkable and happy sight for many
Israelis. The new government of Prime Minister Levi Eshkol
enjoyed 108 votes out of 120 and provided the stable leadership needed in time of war. Public opinion, expressed
largely through press advertisements, was strongly in support of this unity. In 1970 Begin led the Gahal ministers
out of the cabinet in a protest over Israel's policy vis-
à-vis Jarring's mission on behalf of the United Nations.
Gahal maintains that it was a mistake to have even accepted
the possibility of withdrawal from the cease-fire lines,
in the context of peace, while the government kept this
option open, hopefully to facilitate dialogue with the
Arabs. Gahal is supported, often vocally, by the religious
parties in this matter. The differences of opinion were
again aired in the 1969 elections to the Knesset. In these
elections, certain basic principles were common to the
platforms of almost all parties:

1. the safeguarding of Israel's security and sovereignty by strengthening her armed forces, coupled with constant efforts to achieve peace with her neighbors;
2. the maintenance of the cease-fire lines agreed to
by Egypt, Jordan, and Syria in June 1967 until the conclusion of peace treaties specifying secure and recognized
borders, with free navigation in international waterways;
3. the unity of Jerusalem as Israel's eternal capital;
4. close ties with the Jewish people the world over
and with the Zionist movement; an open door for all Jews
able and willing to make their homes in Israel;
5. rapid economic development, progressive social
services, and a fair standard of living for all;
6. extension of secondary and higher education and
advancement of science and technology.

The specific viewpoints of the several parties are
reflected in the following additional points from the programs that they presented at the 1969 polls.

1. Labour-Mapam alignment: the provision of public services, employment, and a livelihood for the Arab population of the newly administered areas and the raising of their economic and social standards; full employment; an increase in the standard of living, especially of less forward groups, and fairer distribution of the national income; a narrowing of the gap in income levels; and the building of a progressive society;

2. Gahal bloc: extension of state sovereignty to the "liberated" areas with Jewish settlement in them; evacuation of the Jews of Iraq, Syria, and Egypt and permission for every Jew of Russia who so desires to settle in the homeland; liberation of the economy from continual dependence on officialdom; obligatory mediation in labor disputes and arbitration in vital public services;

3. National Religious Party: peace treaties based upon the Jewish people's religious and historic right to the Promised Land; no legislation that runs counter to the Laws of the Torah; advancement of religious education and guidance of all schooling by Jewish tradition;

4. Agudat Yisrael: preservation of the unique character of the people of Israel as the people of the Torah; countrywide observance of the sanctity of the Sabbath and Jewish festivals;

5. Poalei Agudat Yisrael: founding of Israel's entire legislation and judicial system on the eternal jurisprudence of the Torah; a plan for the settlement of the Arab refugee question; consolidation and extension of religious farmsteads;

6. Independent Liberals: the establishment of a welfare state in Israel and coexistence of all economic sectors without discrimination; no annexation of territories; economic development in the administered areas; and transfer of Arab refugees from the Gaza strip to Judea, Samaria, and Sinai;

7. National List: integration of the administered areas in the Israeli economy; personal constituency elections to the Knesset and local authorities; uniform state health insurance; free education for ages 3-18;

8. New Communists: full implementation of Security Council Resolution 242 and a foreign policy of peace, neutrality, and friendship with the Soviet Union and all socialist and peace-loving states;

9. Israel Communist Party: defense of Israel's security and sovereignty and her ties with the Jewish people in the Diaspora; political initiative toward a just and permanent peace; recognition of the rights of the Palestinian Arab people;

10.   Free Centre: achievement of permanent peace on
the basis of the preservation of the renewed unity of the
Land of Israel; extensive settlement of the "liberated
areas"; mass immigration to Israel; tax reform and encouragement of private enterprise;

11.   Haolam Hazeh-New Force: peace as Israel's supreme
aim; negotiations between Israel and the Palestine Arab
states to arise in the Land of Israel; free state welfare
services for all.

THE CONSTITUTIONAL PROBLEM

We resolve that, from the moment the Mandate
ends, at midnight on the Sabbath, the sixth of
Iyar 5708, the 15th of May 1948, until the establishment of the duly elected authorities of
the State, in accordance with a Constitution to
be adopted by the elected Constituent Assembly,
not later than 1-10-1948, the National Council
shall act as the provisional Council of State,
and its executive arm, the National Administration, shall constitute the Provisional Government of the Jewish State, and the name of that
State shall be Israel. . . . The State of Israel will rest upon foundations of liberty, justice and peace as envisioned by the prophets of
Israel.   It will maintain complete equality of
social and political rights for all its citizens,
without distinction of creed, race or sex.   It
will guarantee freedom of religion and conscience
of language, education and culture.[4]

Although Israel's Declaration of Independence contains
elements clearly constitutional in character, it does not
in itself constitute a legal document of the type known
elsewhere as the constitution of a country.   The republican
democracy envisaged, with clear echoes of the French and
American revolutions, was a departure both from the Russian
revolutionary background of most of Israel's political
leadership, as well as from the Orthodox Jewish tradition,
which spoke of the eventual restoration of the royal House
of David.   The tyranny of dictatorship was an unpleasant
memory for too many Jewish refugees, and the question of
reviving the monarchy never had been taken seriously, politically speaking.   The immediate traditions of 19th and
20th century Zionism were democratic in nature, and when

in 1947 it became clear that independence was imminent, it
was natural to think in terms of a constitutional republican form of government. The National Council (Vaad Leumi)
appointed a Committee on Constitutional Questions, aided
by legal experts in the community. The Provisional Council
of State, on July 8, 1948, appointed a Constitution Committee, which began studying material for a draft constitution.
Several proposals were tabled (which are of historical interest) and debated by the representatives of the various
parties on the committee. As expected, they expressed
their views in accordance with party doctrine.

The orthodox Agudat Israel stated that "no man-made
Constitution has any place in Israel" and demanded that the
future constitution simply should affirm that the Torah
(Bible) is the constitution of the State of Israel. Other
religious as well as secular groups represented called for
strong emphasis on religious law as an integral part of
the constitution. Socialist speakers stressed the importance of safeguarding social legislation.

Although the committee had debated substantive constitutional matters at length, when the matter was referred to
the Constitution Committee of the First Knesset (well after the deadline of October 1, 1948 set in the Declaration
of Independence), there arose a heated debate whether to
adopt a unified constitution at all or, for the time being,
to make do with a number of basic laws, each of which would
deal, as practical needs might require, with a particular
constitutional feature. The Knesset debated the matter
again in 1950, with Mapai and the religious front opposing
the idea of a unified constitution. This idea was, however,
defended by all other parties, of left, center, and right.
The opposition speakers asserted that the government was
against a constitution because it would alienate religious
support in the coalition and would tend to tie the hands
of the executive. From the government side, the claim was
made that it was not necessary or appropriate for the young
state to bind itself by a rigid constitution, whereas a
nonrigid document would be weak and worthless. After further debate the Knesset resolved to instruct the Constitution, Law and Judicial Committee to prepare a draft constitution composed of separate chapters, each constituting
independent fundamental law. Each such chapter was to be
submitted to the Knesset as and when the committee would
complete its work thereon, and all the chapters together
would form the constitution of the state. Since then, the
Knesset has passed the following basic laws: The Knesset,

Israel Lands, the State President, and the Government. A
fifth basic law dealing with civil rights still is being
drafted. From time to time, parties such as the Independent Liberals or the Gahal bloc voice the need for completing the process of writing Israel's constitution, which
has now gone on for 20 years, but it appears that it yet
will take some time before the final touches are put to
Israel's highest legal text.

NOTES

1. S. D. Johnston, Studies in Asia (Lincoln: University of Nebraska, 1967), pp. 171-172.
2. U. Ulman and R. Linenberg, "Israeli Political Parties and the Decision to Accept German Compensation," State
and Government 1, no. 2 (1971) (Hebrew).
3. M. Levin, "Record of Coalitions," Jerusalem Post,
December 23, 1957.
4. Israeli Declaration of Independence, May 14, 1948.

8

WHERE THE MONEY COMES FROM

As noted by the Israeli scholar E. Guttman,[1] Israeli
party finances are highly centralized, with party headquarters controlling the collection and payment of funds. This
reflects the strong discipline to be found in most of these
parties, which by and large are run from the top down.
Dues and contributions collected locally are transferred
to a central financial department where accounts are kept
and from which all payments are made.

Election financial campaigns are similarly centralized.
Membership dues accounted in the past for between one-third
to two-thirds of party income, according to Guttman. Kibbutz villages (which are all affiliated to one party or
another) pay their dues collectively. Substantial funds
apparently used to reach the parties from the various economic enterprises with which they are connected--financial,
industrial, commercial, and so on. Counterpart parties in
Jewish communities abroad also were said to transfer funds
to the Israeli parties, usually for election campaign purposes. Another source of income was the Histadrut. All
parties of the Histadrut shared in the proceeds of a special "political tax" levied on trade union members--irres-
pective of their personal party affiliation--which was
originally meant to be compulsory, but after adverse public
reactions, was limited to those who did not expressly inform the Histadrut that they objected to being so taxed.
The Histadrut had decided at the end of 1970 to abolish
the arrangement and replace it by a 5.5 percent allocation
of income from dues "to be used for election campaign expenses in the Histadrut and trade unions by the parties

affiliated with the Histadrut, in proportion to their representative strength."

Moab asserted that this was unjust, because his dues that were earmarked originally for social and medical services were being used for political ends. The Histadrut asked the District Court to reject the complaint or transfer it to the competence of a Histadrut Labour Tribunal, arguing that if a member of an organization refused to pay his dues that was a purely internal matter of the organization. The District Court refused to accept the Histadrut point of view, whereupon an appeal was brought by the Histadrut to the Supreme Court. However, here, too, the Histadrut lost its argument and was forcibly reminded of the rule of law by Justice Berinson: "If the Histadrut contentions were to be accepted, this would be tantamount to removing vast areas of human activity from the competence of the national legal system." Pending a District Court decision, the fate of the Histadrut financing of parties is unclear and sub judice.

These resources being still insufficient to meet the high costs of elections in Israel, the Knesset passed the "Knesset and Local Elections--5730--Financing, Limitation of Expenses and Audit Law" of 5729 (1969).[2] Under the terms of this law, parties named in a schedule of the members of the outgoing Knesset were allocated government funds for the financing of election purposes. Transportation of voters, in previous elections a matter of independent party initiative, was in the 1969 poll organized and paid for by the government. Transactions are examined by the state comptroller and expenses are to be kept within the allocations granted. This law was to be the subject of an interesting court action,[3] in which one Dr. Bergman asked the Israeli Supreme Court to restrain the minister of Finance and the state comptroller from acting under its provisions. Bergman complained that the financing law unfairly discriminated against new political parties since it provided government financing only for those parties that were represented in the outgoing Knesset. He won a Court ruling that the Financing Law constituted a "breach of equality of opportunity" for new parties not represented in the retiring Knesset. The opinion indicated that the Knesset might do one of two things: it could either re-enact the Financing Law in its existing form (but by the necessary two-thirds majority that would give it a basic or quasi-constitutional status) or by a simple majority it could amend the law to remove this basic inequality. The Knesset's response was ambiguous. First it amended

the law, on June 22, 1969; the next day it enacted, by a
two-thirds majority, that all legislation pertaining to
elections was valid, thus forestalling any future claims
of invalidity before the Supreme Court.

Commenting on these developments, Bergman has noted
that today political parties in Israel no longer can remain
exempt from state regulation.[4] As recipients of state budgets, the parties technically are agents of the state. By
allocation of election money, by making their expenses subject to state control, the parties' internal decisions on
the election list also have been made part of the electoral
process. At present, internal elections or other arrangements design the party candidates for the Knesset and other
elections. Israeli political parties still maintain the
view that, as associations of persons for political purposes, they need not leave their internal rules and their
application in practice open to supervision by the courts.
However, it seems that in the long run Israeli party leaders will realize that parties may have to choose between
two ways: either to maintain parties as private associations, with internal arrangements open to arbitrary decisions by the ruling groups and give up claim to governmental
budgetary allocations, or to persist in the demand for budgetary allocations, under the law that they themselves
have already voted for and ensure truly democratic decisions within the parties, subject ultimately to control by
the state, through the comptroller and the judiciary.

By 1973, government financing of political parties
had increased considerably, following the passing by the
Knesset on January 24 of the Party Financing Law, 1973.
The Labour Party now received I£ 441,000 a month from the
state budget, with its alignment partner, Mapam, getting
I£ 63,000 a month. On the opposition side, the Gahal bloc
took I£ 234,000 a month, of which Herut was receiving
I£ 135,000. The National Religious Party's share per month
was I£ 108,000. The amounts were reckoned on the basis of
I£ 9,000 per Knesset member. Amounts allocated to the
small parties each month were I£ 36,000 each to Agudat
Yisrael, Independent Liberals, and the State List, I£ 27,000
to the New Communist Party (Rakah), I£ 18,000 each to the
Free Centre, Poalei Agudat Yisrael, and Haolam Hazeh, and
I£ 9,000 to the Israel Communist Party.

The new law provided not only for campaign financing
but also for maintaining the parties between elections.

Election allocations in September 1973 were understood
to be as follows:

Labour Alignment: I£ 6,048,000
Gahal Alignment: I£ 2,808,000
National Religious Party: I£ 1,296,000

The smaller parties were given proportional sums. Apart
from this income from the budget, political party treasur-
ers also could count on the Histadrut subsidies, which had
not been discontinued. While parties were not permitted
under the new law to accept donations from companies or
cooperatives, these traditional sources could be expected
to buy advertising space in party journals. With inflation
affecting the Israeli economy, election expenses in 1973
were expected to be much higher than in 1969.

PARTY POLITICS AND THE PREVENTION OF CORRUPTION IN GOVERNMENT

The establishment of independence brought to power
many party leaders and members and created the problem of
defining the political rights and duties of the civil servant. The Israeli Association of Political Science was invited to draft proposals, which were later incorporated in
the Civil Service Law, 1959. These included the following:

1. A public servant must refrain from any political
or public activity that might harm or might seem to harm
his ability to place the public interest over and above a
party interest or his ability to fulfill his duty equitably.
2. A public servant is particularly enjoined, when
holding senior or representative posts, to refrain from
obvious political activity, including public appearances
on party platforms, participation in demonstrations and
political processions, and participation in political debates in public--orally or in writing.
3. A public servant must refrain from any political
activity while on duty and while in office.
4. A public servant is forbidden to misuse his station for political purposes. He must not try to influence
the political ideas of those working under him or those
with whom he is in touch by virtue of his duty.
5. A public servant is forbidden to collect money
for a political party or group.
6. A public servant is forbidden to utilize party
connections in order to win promotion or extra advantages.
He is forbidden to prefer or discriminate against any
other public servant, to recommend or refrain from recom-

mending, or otherwise determine his behavior toward any other servant on the basis of the similarity or otherwise of political ideas or on the basis of party considerations.

7. A public servant may, as a private individual, express his opinions publicly, orally, or in writing regarding general public issues that do not pertain to his duties, on condition that he is guarded in his style and refrains from criticizing the office in which he is employed, or any other government office, unless so permitted explicitly by his superiors.

NOTES

1. E. Guttman, "Israel," in Comparative Political Finance--A Symposium, ed R. Rose and A. J. Heidenheimer, Journal of Politics 25, no. 3 (1963): 703-717.

2. Law dated February 19, 1969 and published on February 28, 1969 in Official Gazette. Text given in Appendix.

3. N. B. Nimmer, "The Uses of Judicial Review in Israel's Quest for a Constitution," Columbia Law Review 70 (November 1970): 1,221, 1,223 fn. 78.

4. A. A. Bergman, "The Supremacy of the Knesset-- Further Comment on the Election Finance Law Case," Israel Law Review 6, no. 1 (January 1971): 117-126; see also E. Likhovski, Israel's Parliament (Oxford: Clarendon Press, 1971), pp. 60-63.

9

THE 1973
ELECTION YEAR

HISTADRUT, KNESSET, AND MUNICIPALITIES

Four major events occurred in Israel in 1973: the elections to the Histadrut, the Arab assault of Yom Kippur, the Eighth Knesset elections, and the municipal elections.

The Labour Alignment faced constant and chronic internal dissension as it led the nation through crisis after crisis. The component factions of Rafi (led by Defense Minister Moshe Dayan), Ahdut Ha'avoda (led by Deputy Prime Minister Alon), the Mapam Kibbutz group, and the Tel Aviv bloc (Gush) of Mapai (led by Finance Minister Sapir) jostled continuously and were held together mainly by the firm leadership of Prime Minister Golda Meir. In an attempt to reassert left-wing predominance in the Alignment, Histadrut Secretary-General Yitzhak Ben-Aharon won the support of the Mapam and Ahdut Haavoda factions, for ideological reasons, and also enjoyed the pragmatic support of the Rafi group, which for a while threatened to preempt the traditional Mapai control of the Histadrut. The Labour Alignment braved this particular storm and was able to go united to the Histadrut polls on September 11; but the damage had been done and the party declined somewhat--while still retaining its leadership. Ben Aharon quietly handed in his resignation; what was possibly the last attempt to reassert socialist doctrine in the Histadrut passed away. The setback to Golda Meir's party in the Histadrut was an indication of what was yet to come in December, a trend toward the right, which was merely accelerated, but not caused, by the Arab assault of Yom Kippur. Not even labor unity prevented this swing--in fact, it may have precipitated it.

Labour policy statements on the future of Israel-Arab relations went through several revisions both before and after the war, reflecting conflicting schools of thought, with a marked tendency to back-pedal on earlier intentions of intensive Jewish settlement in predominantly Arab regions. Although Mapam registered its disapproval of the right wing of the Alignment (Rafi and Ahdut Haavoda), it stayed in the alliance, hoping to restrain the internal opposition and reluctant to drop out of the government.

Meanwhile, on the right, a challenge emerged in 1973 that, for the first time in Israel's history, had the makings of an alternative government to Labour. Five parties --Herut, the Liberals, the State List, the Free Centre, and the Land of Israel Movement--joined together on September 10 (just in time for the Histadrut elections) to form the Likud (Union) party. The new movement declared its aims:

> To work together for the territorial integrity of the Land of Israel; security and peace; the Return to Zion from countries in which Jews are free to leave, and from those countries from which they must leave; the absorption of immigrants; a social order based on freedom and justice; elimination of poverty and want; the development of an economy that will ensure a decent standard of living for all; the improvement of our environment and the quality of life; the introduction of reforms in local government; and the assurance of democracy by the formation of a strong popular front as an alternative to the ruling party, the Labour Alignment.

This new conservative party grew out of an initiative taken by General Ariel Sharon, former commander of the Southern Command, who was later to distinguish himself on reserve duty in the Yom Kippur War. Sharon formally joined the Liberal Party and established himself as the minister of Defense of the new party's "shadow cabinet," which, not unexpectedly, was headed by the veteran Herut leader, Menachem Begin. Another ex-general, Abraham Yaffe, joined the team on behalf of the Land of Israel movement, as did such former Labour politicians as Yigal Horowitz (State List, ex-Rafi) and Amnon Linn, who under the late Labour Mayor Abba Hushi of Haifa had been active in the party's Arab branch, in that city, but who had been ousted by Hushi's rival, Almogi.

As the 1973 elections drew near, odd things happened in the Arab electorate in Israel. The Orthodox Jewish National Religious Party sought to win orthodox Muslim support by establishing an Arab wing. Tribal sheikhs of Israel's nomad Bedouins decided to establish a party of their own. with the blessing of the Labour Party. The pro-Soviet New Communist Party, deriving most of its strength from Israeli Arab protest votes, placed a Jew (Meir Wilner) at the top of its list, followed by a Greek Orthodox Christian Arab (Tawfiq Toubi) and a Moslem Arab (Tawfiq Ziad) as number three, which had almost been assigned to a Russian Jewish immigrant. Druze villagers were handed leaflets by Druze politicians Hatem Halabi and Amel Nasser-e-Din supporting the Gahal "hard-liners" in their hawkish policy toward the Arab states.

The Bedouin list was the most interesting of these developments. Led by Sheikh Hamad Abu Rabia of the Negev, it also included such tribal leaders as Sheikh Muhammad Hassan Gedeir of Bir Maksur in Galilee, Sheikh Hamzah Saad Zahlaqa of Kafr Qara, and Sheikh Awdah Abu Muammar of the Negev. Thirty-three thousand nomads live in the Negev and 17,000 in Galilee, and this was the first time in history that they were known to have agreed on political unity.

A striking development also occurred in the liberal center, where Shulamith Aloni, a well-known women's leader and civil rights champion, broke with Mapai and formed a new party, the Civil Rights Movement, which resembled the Independent Liberal Party in its platform. For a new party, the Civil Rights Movement was indeed successful, winning three seats in the Knesset elections.

The religious parties were represented by the National Religious Party, minus Shaki (who ran unsuccessfully as an independent), and by the Aguda-Poalei Agudat Yisrael alliance.

On the extreme left, last-minute attempts to patch up endemic disunity were largely unsuccessful. Uri Avneri and his former colleague, Shalom Cohen, sought alliances with assorted New Left and protest groups—colorfully named "Panthers"—but all lost their deposits. The Israel Communist Party, Maki, also found a New Left personality, Meir Pa'il, to lead it and won one seat in the House. The New Communist Party, Rakah, capitalizing on pro-Palestinian and pro-Soviet sentiment among the Arabs of Nazareth and Galilee, was able to secure four seats, but a Maoist list failed.

The Knesset election campaign warmed up during September, after the Histadrut polls (which indicated a Labour setback), and proceeded along traditional lines. Domestic issues were paramount, such as wages, housing, and the cost of living. Foreign policy arguments all proceeded from the assumption that the status quo since the 1967 war would continue without change. On this basis, the "doves" of the left, pointing to the very military strength championed by the "hawks," argued that defense cuts were possible and needed, to meet the rising demands of Israel's consumer society. With the exception of the Communists, <u>not one party</u> thought that Israel should withdraw unilaterally from all territories occupied in the 1967 war. The issue of withdrawal was debated as a theoretical, rather than as a practical, problem. While Mapam and the ILP were inclined to be more reticent and cautious about annexation, other elements within the government, such as Ahdut Haavoda and Rafi, favored the phased settlement of these areas, creating "facts" and bargaining counters for future, and as yet undefined, negotiations. The religious and right-wing opposition generally concurred that to retreat was wrong, either because it was strategically unwise or because it was contrary to divine promises and Jewish responsibilities relating to the Holy Land. These parties generally called for outright annexation of all disputed territories.

And so none of Israel's contesting parliamentarians took into account that the Arab states might try to change the situation. Indeed, from an Egyptian point of view, the wisest course might have been perhaps to encourage, by an appropriate posture of detente, the rise to power in Israel of an extreme left-wing government that would have been amenable to Soviet blandishments and would have concurred readily with Arab demands to give back Sinai, Gaza, Judea, Samaria, the Old City of Jerusalem, and the Golan Heights. Such a weak Israel, led by a pro-Arab government, might then have been pushed even further, to abdicate its very sovereignty in favor of some "Arab Palestine" as envisaged by the Algiers Arab Summit Conference.

However, the Arabs did just the opposite. Ignoring Foreign Minister Eban's eloquent call for an honorably negotiated peace settlement, made at the United Nations on October 3, 1973, the Arab armies of Egypt, Syria, Iraq, Morocco, Algeria, and Kuwait attacked Israel when the nation was at prayer, on October 6, the Day of Atonement (Yom Kippur). From the Pearl Harbor-style assault, ostensibly made to regain lost territories, it seems the Arab invaders had intended to continue, if possible, to the heart of Israel and throw the Jews into the sea. The attack was beaten back at the cost of heavy casualties, among them the Israeli

left wing's prospects of election success. It appears that
Israeli socialist and New Left postures--and their counterparts in the West--had made little impact on Arab thinking.

Not unsurprisingly the war and the shock it engendered
acted as a catalyst on Israeli political processes. The
first practical impact was to cause the postponement of the
Knesset elections to December 31, 1973. Despite the incon-
venience of having most male voters--and many candidates--
under arms, in desert and mountain outposts, Israel was
not going to let foreign aggression prevent her from carry-
ing out her normal democratic processes.

As the public became aware of the military and political events taking place, voices were heard calling for the
reopening of candidate lists and the deferment of elections
until well into 1974. However, this was not accepted by
the larger parties, and so Israel went to the elections
with the same lists as before the war. But, election propaganda now reflected the momentous events of October: the
Labour Alignment appealed to the public to rely on it to
lead the nation to a real peace at the Geneva Conference,
while the Likud opposition made much of the government's
responsibility for the initial military setbacks suffered
by Israel during the first days of the war, before her reserve troops were able to enter the battle and beat back
the enemy. Likud warned against hasty withdrawal from war
gains and expressed deep forebodings about the consequences
of imposed peace agreements. So, the intensity of the war
trauma led many to overestimate possible voter reaction;
in fact, the Israeli public seemed to take the shock in
its stride and, while expressing its feelings of grief and
shock, did not unseat the government. The fundamental stability of Israeli democracy allowed an intense election
campaign to be held under conditions most conducive to the
rise of a Spartan junta, under shellfire and threats of renewed conflict, accompanied by international pressure and
diatribe. Yet, civilians and troops voted in orderly fashion and apparently reflected the sobriety and stolidness
of the nation. Or was it just delayed shock?

A reduced plurality of the people voted again for Golda
Meir's Labour Alignment, which drew most of its support
from the Jewish farmers of the kibbutzim and moshavim, as
well as from the middle-class elements of veteran Israelis
of Ashkenazi origin in the towns and cities. (Meir was
now the oldest member of the Knesset.) But it appeared
that the poor, and many of Israel's new immigrants from
Sephardi communities, preferred the Likud, which grew considerably in the polls. Coming from Arab countries, they

knew what Arab oppression was and supported a party that had declared its "hawkish" stance in defending Israel against Arab imperialism.

The religious parties relied as usual on their traditional support, especially in such orthodox cities as Bnei Brak and Jerusalem, but lost some votes to Likud.

The intelligentsia, of all communities, seemed to be the main supporters of the ILP and the Civil Rights Movement, which formed a natural alliance in the Knesset, while the extreme left, whose "super-dove" platform had been shot down by the Egyptian missiles on the Suez front, failed miserably among Jewish voters.

The biggest surprise came in the municipal elections of Tel Aviv, where Labour was defeated by the Likud candidate, Lahat, who secured his position by an alliance with the ILP. Tel Aviv had been a "safe" Labour seat for many years. In Jerusalem, too, Labour's hold weakened, but Haifa, the industrial port city, gave a landslide victory to its Labour candidate for mayor.

An Israeli political scientist surveying these results predicted that later elections could see the Labour Alignment identified increasingly with the numerically declining Ashkenazi minority and the Likud gaining strength from a combination of the growing Sephardi majority and the anti-left Soviet Jewish immigrants.[1] It would seem, if this prediction is correct, that future Knesset elections eventually will see the emergence of an entirely new leadership, made up largely of new immigrants and representing the communal spectrum of modern Israel far more accurately than the parliaments to date. The trend, already noticed in local government, for new immigrants to reach positions of power will by then extend to Jerusalem; and, with it, the heroic chapter of the founding fathers will come to a close. The sons and daughters of Israel will have come of age.

POSTSCRIPT: SPRING 1974

The Knesset

Shortly after the elections, and well before a new cabinet was formed, the major political parties in the Eighth Knesset apportioned among themselves control of its committees. They agreed that only parties with five or more members in the Knesset would be permitted to choose

which committees they could sit on. Smaller parties would
be simply assigned--or ignored.

Reflecting its increased parliamentary strength, the
Likud Party was given the chairmanship of four committees
and two out of the five deputy speakers of the Knesset.
Likud had hoped to have the chairmanship of the key Finance
Committee or the Defense and Foreign Affairs Committee,
but under a compromise with the Labour Alignment it was
given the following instead: chairmanship of the Education
and Culture, the Economics, the Interior, and the State
Control committees. In the Defense and Foreign Affairs
Committee the Likud was given the newly created post of
permanent deputy chairman, as well as chairmanship of a
joint subcommittee dealing with details of the secret Defense Budget. The National Religious Party was given control of the Constitution, Law and Justice Committee, where
it could ensure the preservation of the status quo regarding religion and state. The Labour Alignment retained
control of all other committees.[2]

Electoral Reform

Electoral reform was a major issue in the spring of
1974, reflecting the general consensus that the present
system was in need of overhauling. On April 3 the Knesset
approved a Labour private member's bill by the minimum absolute majority of 61 votes, enabling further electoral
legislation. The Labour bill presented by Gad Yaacobi also
was supported by the Liberal, Free Centre, and State List
wings of the Likud as well as the Citizens Rights Movement.
The opposing 33 votes came from the Herut wing of the Likud,
the Mapam wing of the Labour Alignment, the Aguda Front,
the National Religious Party, the Independent Liberals, the
New Communists, and the Moked Communists.

Introducing his bill, Yaacobi said the Labour proposal
sought to establish a system in which the voters would know
whom they had chosen and the Knesset member would know who
put him in. Constituency representation would reduce social tensions and heighten popular identification with the
parliament. The parties, when choosing candidates, would
have to take the popular wishes into account more than now,
and the system of checks and balances essential to democracy would be promoted by making the parliament more representative.

Yaacobi said the reform proposal would mean that a voter knew which political program, which particular candidate, and which potential prime minister he was voting for.

Promising that there would be no possibility of turning a minority into a majority, or vice versa, Yaacobi said the dictates of minorities no longer would have the power to deflect national policy. Although he did not presume that his reform would be a miracle cure for the ills of Israeli democracy, it could be a significant step in the right direction.

He said that the Labour Party had wanted a decision in principle about reform, leaving the specifics until later. Its reform entailed the majority of the Knesset members being put in by constituencies on the basis of proportional representation.

Apart from Yaacobi's proposal, which was approved, the Civil Rights Movement, the State List, and the Free Centre all unsuccessfully tabled electoral reform bills of their own, while the Independent Liberal Party also declared it was considering such a move. Another aspect of electoral reform, concerning the internal election procedures of political parties, was dealt with in a private member's bill submitted on April 3 by Dov Zakin of Mapam, with Civil Rights Movement and Moked support. This draft bill provided that candidates for any Knesset or cabinet post, of any party, would be chosen by the largest elected forum of that party in a secret personal ballot and, in a similar procedure, based on local party branches, party candidates would be selected to serve in local government. The draft was couched in general terms to be amplified in subsequent legislation.[3]

Expressing opposition to the Yaacobi reform bill, the Independent Liberal Party said it would distort just representation and ensure the hegemony of a minority. The party cited the effects of the British parliamentary system in which the British Liberal Party recently won only 14 seats, whereas it could have won over 130 had Britain followed the present Israeli system of proportional elections. Noting that the implementation of reform meant the demarcation of constituencies, the ILP warned against the danger of gerrymandering.[4] Other opposing parties felt that the Yaacobi proposals were a continuation of the Bader-Ofer Amendment (see Appendix C) and were designed to eliminate the smaller parties.

The Cabinet

The government in office at the time of the Eighth
Knesset elections, composed of a coalition of the Labour-
Mapam Alignment, the National Religious Party, and the Independent Liberal Party, continued as a caretaker cabinet
until March 10, 1974, when an essentially similar government led again by Golda Meir won a narrow vote of confidence.

The March 10 cabinet, however, proved too fragile and
a month later Meir resigned--and with her the government.

The immediate cause of this instability was the Arab
assault of Yom Kippur. The internal factionalism of both
the Labour and the Religious parties was nothing new; however, the economic and psychological trauma engendered by
the war put Israeli democracy through its severest test
since the country attained independence.

To war veterans returning home, the theological niceties of "Who is a Jew," which caused the two-and-a-half-
month delay in forming the March cabinet, seemed worthy of
postponement, while the unseemly recriminations concerning
responsibility for military unpreparedness prior to the war
did little to enhance national morale.

A respected Commission of Enquiry indeed led to the
cashiering of some senior officers, while the religious
leadership deferred to secular pressure and postponed the
argument for a year. Yet, public pressure on the government, in the form of war veterans' rallies and demonstrations, compelled a split between Defense Minister Dayan (of
Rafi) and his Labour colleagues, and this in turn brought
about Golda Meir's resignation.

Whatever the outcome, it was clear that Israel had
brutally left its adolescence behind and now faced the
serious challenges of adulthood.

NOTES

1. H. Smith, Haaretz, January 8, 1974.
2. Weekly News Bulletin, Government Press Office,
Jerusalem, January 29-February 11, 1974, p. 4.
3. Jerusalem Post, April 4, 1974.
4. Haaretz, April 1, 1974.

At first sight, the most surprising aspect of Israeli parliamentary democracy--with its political parties, news-papers, elections, and free speech--is its very existence. After all, the vast majority of the voters in Israel either were born under the colonial rule of the British Mandate or immigrated from countries where to seek freedom was of-ten to risk one's life, or where elections were empty rit-uals organized from above--if they were to be found at all.

Nor can the question be answered merely by pointing to the traditions of Westminster learned from the British rulers. The same traditions were bequeathed to Canada and Pakistan, to Australia and Nigeria, but the bequest in many ex-colonial lands more often has been honored in the breach than in the observance.

Nor could Israel learn very much from her Arab neigh-bors in this matter--for they, too, only recently have emerged from foreign rule, and not necessarily into forms of democracy. Her ancient Jewish traditions of kingship were too weak to warrant a return to the monarchy of old; indeed, they had become sublimated into the religious--almost mystical--concept of the Messiah, and had been ele-vated out of the realm of secular and mundane politics. Israel therefore, in establishing her modern political life, drew on her cultural patterns and on the experience of Euro-pean nations. From her postbiblical or Talmudical tradi-tions (dating back to before the Middle Ages of Europe), Israel took the principle of debate: within the unity of Jewish religious jurisprudence, the recognized right of any rabbi (teacher) to attempt to persuade his colleagues to accept his interpretations by skillful argumentation (pilpul) created the principle of intellectual pluralism and the avoidance of a single totalitarian dogma. It fol-lowed that so long as a Jew did not expressly exclude him-self from the congregation he was entitled to debate and argue as well as he could. Where the rabbis failed to reach agreement, a consensus usually was reached to post-pone the issue and live with it. Dissent was institutional-ized and rationalized, without threatening the entire framework. Many centuries of this type of religious educa-tion prepared the Jews to accept the principles of parlia-mentarianism and of party differences, while conserving the essential unity of a political framework. Therefore, modern European republican democracy appealed to the founders of the Zionist movement as a pattern to be emulated, and was practically taken for granted almost from the first Zionist Congress.

Another reason for the evolution of parliamentary democracy in Israel was the fact that room had to be found for a broad variety of attitudes and ideas, ranging from the secular to the theocratic, from conservative to radical, from socialist to capitalist. All the various trends, groups, movements, and parties claimed to be equally true to Jewish and Zionist ideals, and it is a tribute to their collective good sense that they decided to search for a modus vivendi along parliamentary lines. Finally, the very small size of the State of Israel (which in its postwar borders is still smaller than Kentucky and only somewhat larger than Maine) has been a contributing factor to the intimacy and immediacy of Israeli political life, which blurs strongly into the social structure. Indeed, Israel's government is intensively and extensively involved, both directly and through its party system, in Israeli society. Yet, there is no real issue of totalitarianism. The accent is still upon growth: Israel's political development has not kept pace with its economic and social progress. It now perhaps is pausing to seek equilibrium, to the hopeful accompaniment of peace with the Arab neighbors, before searching for newer types of political party structures and relationships that will see it safely into the 21st century. (For a broad, yet brief, appraisal, see S. Eisenstadt, "Change and Continuity," Jerusalem Post Magazine, June 1, 1973, p. 11.)

TABLE A.1

Knesset Election Results, 1949-65

Party	First (1-25-1949)		Second (7-30-1951)		Third (7-26-1955)		Fourth (11-3-1959)		Fifth (8-15-1961)		Sixth (11-2-1965)	
	Percentage	Seats	Percentage	Seats	Percentage	Seats	Percentage	Seats	Percentage	Seats	Percentage	Seats
Electorate	506,567		924,885		1,057,795		1,218,483		1,274,280		1,449,709	
Valid votes cast	434,684		687,492		853,219		964,337		1,006,964		1,206,728	
Mapai	35.7	46	37.3	45	32.2	40	38.2	47	34.7	42	44.6	55[a]
Ahdut Haavoda					8.2	10	6.0	7	6.5	8		
Mapam	14.7[b]	19	12.5[b]	15	7.3	9	7.2	9	7.6	9	6.6	8
Herut	11.5	14	6.6	8	12.6	15	13.6	17	13.7	17		
Liberal[c]	5.2	7	18.9	23	10.2	13	6.1	8	13.6	17	21.3[d]	26
	4.1	5	3.2	4	4.4	5	4.6	6			3.8[e]	5
National Religious	12.2	16[f]	8.3	10	9.1	11	9.9	12	9.8	12	8.9	11
Agudat Yisrael			3.7[g]	5	4.7[g]	6	4.7[g]	6	3.7	4	3.3	4
Poalei Agudat Yisrael									1.9	2	1.8	2
Communist	3.5	4	4.0	5	4.5	6	2.8	3	4.1	5	3.4	4[h]
Arab lists[i]	3.0	2	4.7	5	4.9	5	3.5	5	3.5	4	3.3	4
Other	10.1	7[j]	0.7	--	1.9	--	3.4	--	0.7	--	2.9	1[k]

[a] The Mapai Ahdut Haavoda Alignment, with 36.7 percent and 45 seats, and Rafi (7.9 percent and 10 seats).

[b] In 1949 and 1951 Mapam included Ahdut Haavoda.

[c] Figures for first four Knessets refer to General Zionists and Progressives, who merged in 1961 to form the Liberal Party. See also notes d and e.

[d] Herut-Liberal bloc (Gahal).

[e] Independent Liberals.

[f] In 1949 these parties constituted the United Religious Front.

[g] In 1951, 1955, and 1959 these constituted the Torah Religious Front.

[h] Three New Communist List (Rakah) and one Israel Communist Party (Maki).

[i] Associated with or affiliated to Mapai.

[j] Four Sephardim (Mediterranean Jews), one Yemenite Jew, one delegate of the Women's International Zionist Organisation (Wizo) and one of the Freedom Fighters (Lehi).

[k] Haolam Hazeh-New Force.

Seventh Knesset Election Results--October 28, 1969, with State of
Parties at the End of Sixth Knesset

Electorate	1,758,685
Votes	1,427,981
Percentage poll	82
Spoiled votes	60,238
Valid votes cast	1,367,743
Quota per seat[a]	11,274

Party	Seats in End of Sixth Knesset	Votes	Per-cent-age	Seats in Seventh Knesset
Labour-Mapam Alignment (Ma'arach)	63[b]	632,035	46.22	56
Arab lists (pro-Labour)	4	47,989	3.51	4
National (Mamlachti) list	1[c]	42,654	3.11	4
Herut-Liberal bloc (Gahal)	22	296,294	21.67	26
Free Centre[d]	4	16,393	1.20	2
Independent Liberals	4[e]	43,933	3.21	4
National Religious Party	11	133,238	9.74	12
Agudat Israel	4	44,002	3.22	4
Poalei Agudat Yisrael	2	24,968	1.83	2
New Communist list (Rakah)	3	38,827	2.84	3
Israel Communist Party (Maki)	1	15,712	1.15	1
Haolam Hazeh (New Force)	1	16,853	1.23	2
Land of Israel list[f]	--	7,591	0.55	--
Peace list[f]	--	5,138	0.37	--
Young Israel[f]	--	2,116	0.15	--

[a]Obtained by deducting the votes cast for lists gaining less
than 1 percent of the total and dividing the remainder by 120.
One hundred and fourteen seats were allocated for complete multi-
ples of the quota, and the rest to the six lists with the largest
remainders.

[b]Mapai-Ahdut Haavoda Alignment, 9 of Rafi, 8 Mapam, and 1
Independent Liberal (see c and e).

[c]David Ben Gurion.

[d]Independent faction formed after a split in Gahal.

[e]One left to join Israel Labour Party (Avizohar).

[f]Obtained less than 1 percent each of valid votes cast in
1969 election.

Note: There were slight changes over the past four years in
voting strength in the Seventh Knesset not represented in this
table. The changes came about when three MKs split from their
parties. Shalom Cohen broke away from Haolam Hazeh (now Meri)
and led the new Black Panther list; Avner Shaki split from the
National Religious Party as an independent; and Meir Avizohar
broke away from the State List to join forces with Labour.

TABLE A.3

The Eighth Knesset Elections, December 31, 1973

Party	Votes	Seats
Labour Alignment (Ma'arach)	621,183	51
National Religious Party (Mafdal)	130,349	10
Aguda Poalei Agudat Yisrael	60,012	5
New Communists (Rakah)	53,353	4
Black Panthers	13,332	0
Union (Likud)	473,309	39
Cooperation and Brotherhood	9,949	0
Jewish Defense League	12,811	0
Independent Liberals	56,560	4
Movement for Social Equality (Shaki)	10,202	0
Popular Movement	1,101	0
Arab Bedouin list (pro-Labour)	16,408	1
Brotherhood Movement	4,433	0
Arab Israeli list	3,269	0
Blue and White Panthers	5,945	0
Moked (Communists)	22,147	1
Progress and Development (Arab list) (pro-Labour)	22,604	2
Yemenites	3,195	0
Socialist Revolutionary list	1,201	0
Civil Rights Movement	35,023	3
Meri (Haolam Hazeh)	10,469	0
Total	1,566,855	

Note: Out of 21 contending parties, 11 failed to win even 1 seat. Out of 2,037,478 enfranchised voters, 1,601,098 voted, and of these votes, 34,243 were declared invalid. Compare Table 9 for unsuccessful parties in the Fourth Knesset.

Source: Official Gazette, January 11, 1974.

TABLE A.4

Eighth Knesset Election: Breakdown by Townships

Township	Vote	Align-ment	Likud	NRP	Aguda	ILP	Rakah	Meri	Moked	Black Pan-thers	Aloni	League
				The Urban Knesset Vote								
Jerusalem	--	12,420	17,932	3,813	4,237	1,368	183	263	735	373	1,149	795
Tel Aviv	--	21,024	18,348	3,166	1,541	2,709	562	465	933	270	1,453	353
Haifa	--	81,308	50,967	11,789	5,437	9,085	3,668	1,208	2,480	1,337	4,899	1,042
Acre	--	4,767	3,383	802	613	201	1,866	26	83	216	63	58
Afula	--	2,548	1,361	561	214	132	5	18	37	22	97	17
Arad	--	1,104	691	47	28	112	9	13	47	18	133	5
Ashdod	--	2,129	1,741	463	291	109	11	28	27	110	84	23
Ashkelon	--	2,128	1,392	854	210	133	6	12	28	37	56	56
Bat Yam	--	20,659	16,302	2,817	556	1,492	248	266	879	375	1,050	236
Beersheba	--	3,478	2,829	1,082	649	248	23	35	75	193	149	62
Bnei Brak	--	7,446	8,498	5,884	9,290	514	144	88	211	213	229	1,195
Carmiel		315	115	14	1	13	3	--	5	5	8	6
Hadera	--	1,979	1,382	602	107	141	4	11	39	47	86	18
Herzliya	--	5,831	4,678	1,544	432	841	42	118	224	107	468	77
Holon	--	9,890	7,017	1,162	224	825	66	133	366	185	499	95
Kfar Saba	--	2,471	1,458	347	63	146	9	18	28	39	113	22
Lod	--	5,659	3,970	786	679	195	283	33	68	150	150	91
Netanya	--	13,022	10,699	3,773	1,428	1,371	83	114	312	350	506	264
Petah Tikva	--	6,503	5,364	1,938	844	454	66	109	151	124	210	184
Ramle	--	4,989	4,496	1,582	182	370	687	53	124	168	107	76
Safad	--	2,179	1,573	532	433	217	4	18	26	46	66	156
Tiberias	--	3,815	2,464	1,254	974	307	8	49	34	61	69	82
Ramat Gan	62,277	24,453	23,572	4,239	916	2,937	255	525	835	375	1,905	443
				The Rural Knesset Vote								
Adamit (k) A	--	60%	5%						30%		5%	
Aminadav (m) TM	97/65%	44.7%	38.3%	11.6%		1.1%			1.1%	2.1%	1.1%	1.1%

Settlement	Reg./Turnout									
Avihail (m) TM	--	217	46	13		11		3	3	15	2
Beer Tuvia (m) TM	--	283	53	2		16		3	3	3	
Beit Alfa (k) A	383/73%	88.7%	1%	2.1%		0.3%					
Beti Zayit (m) TM	--	139	67	7		10		7	2	10	
Ein Shemer (k) A	310/74%	96.8%	0.3%	0.3%					2.9%		
Gadot (k) M	--	98				5			4		
Gan Shmuel (k) A	373/68%	78.8%	0.5%			1.1%		0.5%	16.8%	1.6%	
Ginnosar (k) M	--	95.9%	0.9%					0.4%	0.5%	2.3%	
Hamadiya (k) I	--	87%	10%							3%	
Kfar Habad (m)	--	4	55	449							29
Kfar Vitkin (m) TM	--	80.4%	10.9%	0.2%	2	3.8%		0.2%	0.4%	2.1%	0.2%
Moaz Hayim (k) M	--	99%	1%								
Merhavia (k) A	--	259						3	15	6	
Mishmar Ha'emek (k) A	410/74%	96.1%	4%			1.7%			2.2%		
Moledet (m) TM	232/76%	86.5%				5.2%			1.7%		
Na'an (k) M	523/72%	95.1%	1%			1%			1.6%	0.6%	
Nezer Sereni (k) I	301/63.5%	85.8%	4.4%	0.5%		5.1%	0.3%	0.7%	1%	2%	
Ramat Yohanan (k) I	--	269	13	2		4			4	3	1
Revivim (k) I	--	188	3	1		2			19	3	
Sa'ad (k) D	--	7	36	156							
Sde Eliezer (m) OZ	--	29	31	4		41				2	1
Shavei Zion (m) IH	203/57%	41.8%	19.9%	15.9%		14.9%					
Shoresh (m) OZ	--	6	6			63					
Tel Adashim (m) TM	200/74.5%	53.3%	35.7%	1.5%		6%		1.5%	0.5%	1	0.5%
Tel Yosef (k) I	--	278	8	5		1			1	9	
Tirat Zvi (k) D	--	5%	5%	90%						1	
Udim (m) IH	--	66			2	10					
Yad Hanna (k) M	--	6	1	1	3	1		1	36	6	57
Yagur (k) M	327/72.5%	312	1	1	1	1		1	4	3	

k = kibbutz   m = moshav   A = Artzi   I = Ihud   M = Meuhad

TM = Tnuat Ha'Moshavim   OZ = Ha'Oved Ha'Zioni   D = Ha'kibbutz Ha'Dati   IH = Ihud Haklai

Note: Complete, official returns had not been published by April 1974. The voting figures here were derived from press reports, and are given sometimes as totals and sometimes as percentages of the total vote cast.

TABLE A.5

Histadrut Elections, 1956-73
(percentages of votes won, by party)

Party	1956	1959	1969	1973
Labour Alignment				
Mapai	57.74	55.43 ⎞		
Ahdut Haavoda	14.61	17.03 ⎬	62.11	58.35
Mapam	12.54	13.92 ⎠		
Union (Likud)				
General Zionists	3.81	3.48 ⎞	16.58 ⎞	
Herut	--	-- ⎠		22.69
Free Centre	--	--	1.99 ⎬	
State List	--	--	3.85 ⎠	
Progressives (Independent Liberals)	5.25	5.77	5.69	5.97
Religious Workers	1.96	1.79	3.06	4.27
New Force (Meri)	--	--	1.33	0.75 (failed)
Communists (Moked) ⎞			1.79	1.73
Communists (Rakah) ⎠	4.09	2.79	2.25	2.38
Black Panthers	--	--	--	1.63
Friendship list	--	--	0.54	0.91
Independents	--	--	--	0.32
Leftist alliance	--	--	0.54	0.27 (failed)
Yemenites "A"	--	--		0.42
Yemenites "B"	--	--	1.08	0.31

Note: Trends discernible from this table are: (1) the decline of Labour despite its unification; (2) the growing strength of nonsocialist elements of the Union inside the avowedly socialist Histadrut; and (3) the appearance of a variety of small protest groups within the establishment.

Comparative Histadrut Party Strengths on a Geographic Basis, 1973

Town	Vote	Align-ment	Likud	Inde-pen-dent Lib-erals	Reli-gious Work-ers	Moked	Meri	Black Pan-thers	Rakah
Jeru-salem	43,563	21,035	14,099	2,980	2,407	832	409	966	267
Tel Aviv	--	56.39	25.29	7.02	4.37	--	0.98	1.40	1.18
Haifa	111,000	56.61	26.00	6.93	3.36	1.76	0.90	1.30	1.46
Acre	8,653	56.32	23.23	2.21	4.31	0.70	0.34	4.07	7.48
Afula	5,631	52.31	28.88	4.24	8.01	0.78	0.83	2.54	0.27
Arad	1,918	61.12	19.55	11.36	1.46	2.60	1.04	1.20	0.31
Ashdod	8,432	57.42	27.10	3.76	6.38	0.60	0.58	2.50	0.39
Ashke-lon	8,495	57.60	24.13	5.47	8.95	--	0.64	2.16	--
Bat Yam	21,223	56.01	27.70	4.67	3.49	3.31	0.88	1.64	0.77
Beer-sheba	15,710	53.53	21.47	5.20	7.49	1.59	1.05	7.83	0.44
Bnei Brak	9,935	53.66	23.58	3.31	7.27	2.13	0.69	2.18	1.52
Carmiel	1,774	68.32	20.67	4.90	0.45	0.79	0.67	0.56	2.53
Dimona	4,978	55.28	27.08	6.51	1.18	0.58	0.70	7.27	0.16
Eilat	--	55.32	31.00	4.86	2.13	0.69	2.95	1.63	0.22
Hadera	10,114	59.09	23.26	5.75	4.42	1.31	0.53	3.35	0.22
Herz-liya	11,084	58.66	23.89	12.32	5.13	--	--	--	--
Holon	25,868	55.39	25.37	6.62	4.12	2.97	0.88	1.66	0.60
Kfar Saba	9,963	57.95	25.61	4.23	3.72	--	--	--	--
Lod	9,375	48.65	23.68	3.05	6.12	0.58	0.57	11.35	1.28
Naha-riya	9,422	62.26	20.69	6.38	3.51	0.63	0.48	1.01	3.63
Netanya	15,583	54.10	19.27	8.97	9.17	1.66	0.56	3.84	0.46
Naza-reth	6,075	52.66	4.23	4.28	0.32	0.45	0.10	0.57	36.66
Petah Tikva	27,849	57.61	23.65	4.44	4.89	1.40	0.75	1.91	0.75
Ramle	8,833	46.59	21.62	5.57	8.81	1.40	0.40	1.50	3.54
Rishon	16,434	60.12	26.04	5.06	3.23	1.35	0.95	1.18	0.50
Safad	3,610	67.86	16.84	7.81	2.69	0.55	0.58	1.27	1.10
Tiberias	6,613	59.67	25.09	4.62	5.18	0.55	0.42	1.09	2.37
Zichron	1,983	68.06	24.91	1.81	1.82	0.25	0.10	0.95	1.15

1973 Municipal Election Results (Major Cities)

Jerusalem
Voted: 102,139 (50.5%)*

Alignment	42.2%
Likud	21.6%
Aguda	12.9%
National Religious	11.3%
Independent Liberals	3.1%
Independent Merchants list	2.5%
Iraqi Immigrants	2.1%
Black Panthers	1.7%
Jewish Defense League	1.5%
Citizens for a Better Jerusalem	1.1%

Ashkelon
Voted: 4,509 (65%)

Alignment	39.8%
Likud	25.9%
National Religious	23.2%
Aguda	3.2%
Independent Liberals	2.6%

Bat Yam
Voted: 46,146 (65.5%)

Alignment	44.7%
Likud	36.4%
National Religious	9.2%
Aguda	1.3%
Rakah	0.6%
Moked	2.0%
Black Panthers	1.0%
Local list	0.5%

Eilat
Voted: 5,091 (49%)

Alignment	51.4%
Likud	36.7%
National Religious	7.9%
Independent Liberals	4.0%

Hadera
Voted: 15,481

Alignment	5,431
Likud	6,255
National Religious	2,365
Independent Liberals	734
Black Panthers	346

Haifa

Alignment	58.4%
Likud	19.7%
National Religious	6.9%
Aguda	3.6%

Haifa (continued)

Independent Liberals	5.1%
Rakah	2.9%
Moked	2.8%
Black Panthers	1.0%

Acre
Voted: 66.6%

Alignment	37.5%
Likud	10.9%
Aguda	9.7%
Independent Liberals	1.0%
Rakah	10.6%
Arab list	5.4%
Black Panthers	3.0%
Arab list	16.5%

Herzliya
Voted: 20,321 (67%)

Alignment	8,309
Likud	6,208
National Religious	2,508
Aguda	782
Independent Liberals	1,573
Ahva	217
Local list	264

Kiryat Shmona
Voted: 5,806 (64.5%)

Alignment	1,174
Likud	386
National Religious	575
Aguda	447
Independent Liberals	121
Local list	2,834

Kfar Saba
Voted: 13,609 (70%)

Alignment	8,527
Likud	2,439
National Religious	1,726
Aguda	246
Independent Liberals	356

Lydda
Voted: 13,168 (63%)

Alignment	5,20
Likud	3,04
National Religious	73
Aguda	68
Independent Liberals	19
Rakah	30
Three local lists	2,66

Nahariya
Voted: 12,367 (67%)

Alignment	5,014
Likud	1,707
National Religious	876
Aguda	328
Independent Liberals	485
Black Panthers	335
Local list	3,388

Netanya
Voted: 33,738 (64%)

Alignment	9,256
Likud	9,407
Two local religious lists	8,513
Independent Liberals	2,478
Social Equality	804
Ahva	1,233
Two local lists	1,227

Petah Tikva
Voted: 45,946 (69%)

Alignment	15,725
Likud	11,436
National Religious	5,796
Ahva	2,625
Independent Liberals	1,791
Yemenite list	3,575
Black Panthers	693
Two local lists	3,607

Ramat Gan
Voted: 62,200 (69%)

Alignment	24.2%
Likud	43.3%
Religious lists	8.2%
Independent Liberals	4.4%
Rakah	0.5%
Ahva	7.4%
Local list	12.1%

Ramle
Voted: 14,587 (65%)

Alignment	4,091
Likud	2,240
National Religious	3,165
Two local lists	1,516
Independent Liberals	546
Rakah	540
Ahva	1,598
Black Panthers	101
Arab list	460

Tel Aviv

Alignment	33.2%
Likud	42.9%
National Religious	6.2%
Aguda	3.5%
Independent Liberals	5.4%
Rakah	0.9%
Eddie Malka	1.8%
Moked	1.4%
Black Panthers	0.9%
Social Equality	0.4%
Local list	3.6%

Tiberias
Voted: 9,690 (69%)

Alignment	3,058
Likud	1,497
National Religious	1,601
Aguda	1,017
Independent Liberals	825
Meri	71
Black Panthers	100
Three local lists	1,326

Zichron Yaacov
Voted: 5,487 (56%)

Alignment	1,649
Likud	822
National Religious	556
Aguda	334
Independent Liberals	271
Rakah	64
Local list	1,672

*These figures represent, respectively, the total vote and percentage of eligible electorate voting. Data for some municipalities are incomplete.

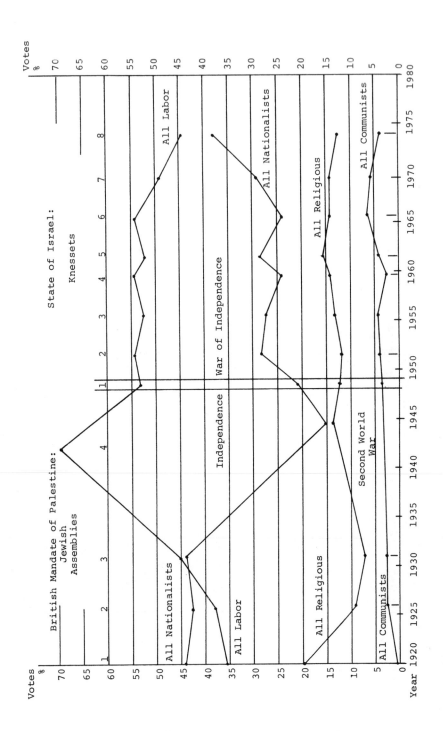

CHART

Fifty Years of Free Elections

The chart summarizes the election results for the
four Assemblies in Mandatory times and the eight Knessets
of independent Israel. The resulting panorama of 12 elections in 50 years shows some very clear trends.

Whereas the labor movement was only in its infancy
in the 1920s, it quickly overtook the nonlabor segment of
the Jewish population, which at that time was predominantly
urban and Sephardi in character ("the old yishuv"). The
decline in apparent religious and nationalist strength during the Mandate is explained by their boycott of the labor-
dominated national institutions, a breach of national unity
that during the late 1940s almost reached the point of
civil war. However, since independence, all political
forces have participated in the elections. While labor
retained its position throughout, it appears to be declining since the 1965 elections, with the graph showing a
floating vote moving alternately left and right, latterly
favoring the nationalists. Both the religious and communist movements have been fairly static throughout and do
not reflect much change in their relative strengths. In
order to simplify the complex patterns of Israeli parties,
"Labour" denotes all factions that eventually became part
of the Alignment, "Nationalists" denotes all factions of
the liberal and right wings, "Religious" incorporates all
factions of that designation, and so with "Communists."

APPENDIX B
COMPOSITION OF THE
MARCH 1974 CABINET

COMPOSITION OF THE MARCH 1974 CABINET

Labour Ministers

Mapai

Prime Minister	Golda Meir
Agriculture	Haim Gvati
Finance	Pinhas Sapir
Foreign Affairs	Abba Eban
Housing	Yehoshua Rabinowitz
Justice	Haim Zadok
Labour	Yitzhak Rabin
Police	Shlomo Hillel
Transport	Aharon Yariv
Communications	Aharon Uzan
Commerce and Industry	Haim Bar Lev

Ahdut Ha'avoda

Deputy Prime Minister	Yigal Alon
Without portfolio	Israel Galili

Mapam

Health	Victor Shemtov
Immigrant Absorption	Shlomo Rosen

Rafi

Defense	Moshe Dayan
Information	Shimon Peres

National Religious Party Ministers

Interior	Yosef Burg
Religious Affairs	Yitzhak Raphael
Social Welfare	Michael Hazani

Independent Liberal Party Ministers

Tourism	Moshe Kol
Without portfolio	Gideon Hausner

Document   Page

 1. League of Nations Mandate for Palestine, 1922   132

 2. United Nations Resolution 181(11) on the
     Palestine Question, November 29, 1947   132

 3. Transition Law, 5709 (1949), Chapter One--
     The Knesset   132

 4. Basic Law: The Knesset, 1958   133

 5. Basic Outline of the Government Programme
     (Coalition Agreement), March 8, 1949   133

 6. Basic Principles of the Government Programme
     Approved by the Knesset, 1959 (Excerpts)   139

 7. Basic Law: The Government, 1968 (Excerpts)   140

 8. Knesset and Local Authorities Elections (5730)
     (Financing, Limitation of Expenses, and Audit),
     Law 5729 (1969)   142

 9. The Party Financing Law, 1973   147

10. The Bader-Ofer Amendment   150

11. Notice Regarding the Secrecy and Honesty of
     the Elections--Elections Law (Electioneering
     Methods), 1959   151

12. Election Propaganda, 1948, 1969, 1973   154

        1948 Election Propaganda   154
        1969 Election Propaganda   159
        1973 Election Propaganda   172

1. League of Nations Mandate for Palestine, 1922

Article 2

The Mandatory shall be responsible for placing the country under such political, administrative and economic conditions as will secure the establishment of the Jewish National Home, as laid down in the preamble, and the development of self-governing institutions, and also for safeguarding the civil and religious rights of all the inhabitants of Palestine, irrespective of race and religion.

Article 3

The Mandatory shall, so far as circumstances permit, encourage local autonomy.

2. United Nations Resolution 181(11) on the Palestine Question, November 29, 1947

Part 1, Paragraph B, Partition Plan, Article 9

The Provisional Council of Government of each State (the Israeli and Palestinian) shall, not later than two months after the withdrawal of the armed forces of the Mandatory power, hold elections to the Constituent Assembly which shall be conducted on democratic lines.

Article 10(a)

Establishing in each state a legislative body elected by universal suffrage and by secret ballot on the basis of proportional representation, and an executive body responsible to the legislature.

3. Transition Law, 5709 (1949), Chapter One--The Knesset

Article 1

The legislative body of the State of Israel shall be called the Knesset. The Constituent Assembly shall be

called the First Knesset. A delegate to the Constituent
Assembly shall be called a member of the Knesset.

Article 2(a)

An enactment of the Knesset shall be called a law.

4. Basic Law: The Knesset, 1958

1. The Knesset is the parliament of the State.
2. The seat of the Knesset is Jerusalem.
3. The Knesset shall, upon its election, consist of
120 members.
4. The Knesset shall be elected by general, national,
direct, equal, secret and proportional elections, in accordance with the Knesset elections law. This section shall
not be changed save by a majority of the members of the
Knesset.

5. Basic Outline of the Government Programme
(Coalition Agreement), March 8, 1949

Section I: Collective Responsibility

The Government is formed on the basis of collective
responsibility binding on all its members and on all its
constituent parties. This collective responsibility covers
the agreed programme of the Coalition and all Cabinet divisions. It does not bar members of the Knesset from free
discussion of any proposal that comes up for consideration
or the free criticism of the Government should it depart
from the policy laid down by the Knesset or agreed upon by
the Coalition.

Section II: Liberty, Equality and Democracy

The democratic republican regime of the State of Israel shall guarantee by law complete equality of rights
and obligations for all citizens regardless of creed, race,
or nationality. It shall safeguard freedom of religion,
freedom of conscience, freedom of language, education, and
culture. It shall establish full equality of rights and
obligations for women--civic, social, economic, and legal.
Freedom of association and freedom of expression, verbal
and written, shall be guaranteed, with due regard for the

133

security of the State, its liberty and independence, and with consideration for the rights of others. In elections to all State, Municipal, and other representative bodies, franchise shall be universal without distinction of sex, creed, race or nationality and without financial qualification. The State shall provide for the public religious needs of its inhabitants but shall prevent religious coercion. The Sabbath and Jewish Festivals shall be fixed as days of rest in the State of Israel; non-Jews shall have the right to observe their own Sabbaths and festivals as days of rest.

Section III: Foreign Policy

The foreign policy of Israel shall be based on the following principles:

1. Loyalty to the fundamental principles of the United Nations' Charter and friendship with all peace-loving States and especially with the USA and the USSR.
2. Efforts to achieve an Arab-Jewish Alliance based on economic, social, cultural, and political cooperation with the neighbouring countries. This Alliance must be within the framework of the United Nations, and cannot be directed against any of its members.
3. Support for all measures which strengthen peace, guarantee the rights of man and the equality of nations and enhance the authority and effectiveness of the United Nations Organisation.
4. The right of all Jews, who wish to resettle in their historic homeland, to leave the countries of their present abode.
5. The effective preservation of the complete independence and sovereignty of Israel.

Section IV: Security

General military service. Age groups and methods shall be specified by law.

Section V: Immigration

1. The ingathering of the Exiles.
2. The attraction of immigrants to rural areas and to all forms of agricultural settlement; the establishment of training farms and the provision of experienced guidance by veteran farmers to immigrants in new settlement enterprises.

3. Provision of vocational training to immigrants and the fostering of crafts and cooperative methods.

4. Assistance for the absorption of immigrants in all branches of economic life.

5. The provision of housing for immigrants.

6. Facilities for immigrants to learn Hebrew and become integrated into the cultural, economic and social life of the country.

Section VI: Development Plan

The Government shall draw up a Four Year Development and Absorption Plan aimed at doubling the country's population in this period through mass immigration and intensive development on the basis of a planned economy with the following objectives:

1. The speedy settlement of all under-populated areas, a balanced distribution of population and prevention of over-crowding in the cities.

2. Efforts to develop Jerusalem by the concentration of cultural, national, and governmental institutions, the exclusive siting of certain enterprises in Jerusalem, the transfer of certain industries to this city, and the creation of a network of villages around and in the area connecting it with the Shfelah and the coastal plain. The economic consolidation of Safed and Tiberias shall also be the subject of special effort.

3. Irrigation of the valleys and the Negev, afforestation, swamp drainage, soil improvement and agricultural development in all parts of the country.

4. The nationalisation of the sources of water and of natural resources of water and of natural resources; of desolate areas of land and of services on which the security of the State depends. No property shall be requisitioned or confiscated without adequate compensation.

5. The obligatory development of all derelict lands, whether by transfer to a State development authority or by the instrument of special taxation.

6. The encouragement of private capital and of private and cooperative initiative in town and country; inducement for the investment of capital in productive enterprises assisting the speedy and effective development of the country's natural resources and economic capacities; facilities for the transfer of Jewish capital from the Diaspora.

7. Efforts to establish labour settlements in country and town and expand all forms of settlement and labour

cooperation with the preservation of freedom of the individual to choose the form of settlement in which he wishes to live.

8. Efforts to improve telephone, telegraph, and radio services and to develop land, air, and sea communications within the country and with all parts of the world.

9. A systematic campaign against the high cost of living while preserving decent living conditions for the workers and popular masses through the following means:

(a) Effective control of imports and prices of imported goods, costs of production and prices of local industrial and agricultural products, and of transport and service charges.

(b) Narrowing the margins of profit and the exaggerated returns of the middle man.

(c) Strict control of the use of foreign exchange; the encouragement of the import of those means of production which can strengthen our agricultural and industrial productive capacity and reduce costs; priority in the import of essential foodstuffs, fuel, building materials, equipment and the productive means to expand the country's economy.

(d) The introduction of an austerity regime during the transition period by the strict rationing of food, clothing, and other essential commodities and the imposition of severe penalties for all forms of speculation, particularly in housing and on profiteering and black-marketeering.

(e) The rationalisation of production and the improvement of equipment designed to increase output and quality and to lower prices; organised marketing; advanced technical training for workers; increase in the productivity of labour by improving conditions; cheapening of credit; increased self-sufficiency; and expansion of production for export.

10. The rehabilitation and expansion of the citrus industry, improvement of labour methods in the industry, and assistance for the marketing of its products abroad.

11. The wide use of all modern scientific and technical methods for the promotion of the country's economy, of its general and technical education, and for the quantitative increase and qualitative improvement of production.

12. Exemption from and reduction of taxation and customs duties designed to encourage private and cooperative investments in development projects in agriculture, indus-

try, maritime and building enterprises, particularly in desolate and neglected regions.

13. The imposition of progressive income tax, luxury and inheritance taxes, and taxes on increments from raised property values, with the object of assuring a fair distribution of the burden of maintaining security and State Services.

14. A tariff and foreign trade policy aimed at the encouragement and promotion of local industry and agriculture.

15. The gradual systematic improvement of the standard of living, standards of education, labour and health for all sections of the population, regardless of nationality, community, and sex.

16. The eradication of illiteracy, overcrowding, and disease in the slums.

17. The removal of communal barriers in social and civic life.

18. The progressive introduction of a wide social insurance scheme for the entire population against sickness, old age, widowhood and infirmity.

19. The speeding up of building to meet the housing needs of the immigrants and to clear the slums.

20. The encouragement of the birth rate by the provision of grants and special allowances to large families.

21. The encouragement of Jewish and other tourists by the promotion of the hotel industry and the establishment of effective services for the overseas dissemination of information about our country, its antiquities, its beauty spots, and its economic possibilities.

Section VII: Education

The establishment of a special Ministry for Education and Culture to provide a general education for all children; assure a decent cultural level for every man and woman in Israel; enable all immigrants to acquire a knowledge of the Hebrew language; make available in Hebrew the world's literary treasures; encourage literature, science and the arts; promote pure and applied research in the natural sciences; integrate culturally and socially immigrants from all parts of the world; attract to this country Jews with universal prominence in science, Torah studies, literature and the arts; disseminate among Jews a knowledge of the Middle East and the Arab people; safeguard the right of all Arab citizens of the State to use Arabic as the language of instruction, with Hebrew as a language of study.

Education shall be free for all boys and girls up to
an age to be fixed by law. School attendance shall be compulsory for all children. Agricultural and technical education shall be expanded and the youth educated to a life
of labour. Scholarships shall be provided to enable tal-
ented children to continue their studies in secondary
schools and universities. An obligatory minimum and standard curriculum shall be drawn up for all recognised auton-
omous school systems and all other schools. For Jewish
schools this curriculum shall comprise the Hebrew language,
Jewish and general history, local and general geography,
the Bible and Hebrew literature, the sciences, a branch of
manual labour or craft in agriculture or industry, physical training, pioneering values, and civics. In Arab
schools suitable adaptations shall be made.

The Government will encourage and foster the pioneering
Youth Movements in the fulfillment of their task in agricultural settlement and in all spheres of labour pioneering.

Section VIII: Ex-Servicemen's Resettlement

Ex-servicemen in permanent employment before joining
the Army shall be entitled by law to return to their former
places of occupation. Ex-servicemen shall enjoy priority
in securing employment; ex-servicemen with no profession
or craft before joining the Army shall be given the chance
to learn a trade; ex-servicemen shall be helped to join or
create any form of agricultural settlement and shall receive loans for housing and economic rehabilitation; all
men whose academic training was interrupted by Army service
shall be assisted to continue their studies; among ex-servicemen priority shall be given to war invalids in employment and in facilities for earning their livelihood.

The State shall assume responsibility for families
whose bread winners fell in the war or were deprived of
their working capacity as a result of the war.

Section IX: Labour Legislation

The State shall guarantee freedom of association for
workers and shall encourage the creation of an all-embrac-
ing trade union comprising all workers; it shall lay down
minimum wage rates in various occupations; it shall encourage the principle of collective bargaining; it shall
guarantee the right to strike and shall create machinery
for mediation to prevent labour disputes; it shall set up
by progressive stages a network of institutions for social

insurance and mutual help against unemployment, accident,
infirmity, old age, orphanage, and widowhood; it shall introduce safety laws for industrial labourers, legislation
for proper sanitary and hygienic conditions in places of
work and for the right to holidays and days of rest; the
Government shall secure for Arab workers equal rights with
Jewish workers through a constructive policy aimed at the
progressive rise in the standard of living, organisation,
education, and culture of the Arab worker to the level of
the Jewish worker.

Working youth shall be given vocational training;
evening classes shall be established where they may continue their general educations.

The law shall prohibit the employment of women in
trades injurious to motherhood; women shall receive mater-
nity leave with pay and shall enjoy the right to return to
their jobs; night work for mothers shall be prohibited.
There shall be strict control of the employment of young
persons between the ages of 15 and 18, while the employment
of children up to and including the age of 14 shall be prohibited. There shall be equal pay for equal work for men
and women.

Special institutions shall be established for the
welfare and education of children of women working away
from their homes.

A united labour exchange shall distribute employment
to all persons in need of work without any discrimination
on grounds of community, nationality, party affiliation,
or any other consideration, in accordance with legislation
to be instituted.

Section X: Civil Service

The Government considers it necessary to introduce a
system of civil service appointment on the basis of exam-
inations to be conducted by an independent commission.

6. Basic Principles of Government Programme
Approved by the Knesset, 1959 (Excerpts)

Chapter One: Collective Responsibility

1. Collective responsibility applies to all members
of the Cabinet and to all the parties participating in the
Government. The Basic Principles and the decisions of the
Cabinet are obligatory on all the members of the Cabinet

and their parties. Abstention from voting in the Knesset
on the Cabinet's decisions is permissible only with the
Cabinet's approval, or after resignation from the Cabinet
before the vote.
   2. The parties have complete freedom on the question
of the electoral system.
   3. The following amendment to the Transition Law will
be submitted to the Knesset:

> Collective responsibility is obligatory for the
> members of the Cabinet and the representatives
> of their parties in the Knesset. A vote in the
> Knesset by a member of the Cabinet or the repre-
> sentatives of his party in the Knesset against
> a decision of the Cabinet, or abstention from
> voting in the Knesset by a member of the Cabinet
> or the representatives of his party in the Knes-
> set on a decision of the Cabinet without the Cab-
> inet's permission, shall be equivalent to the
> resignation of that member of the Cabinet. This
> resignation shall take effect on its announce-
> ment by the Prime Minister in the Knesset. The
> announcement shall not require the approval of
> the Knesset.

   58. No party propaganda will be permitted among the
pupils in State schools of all kinds.
   61. The Government will prevent any religious or anti-
religious coercion from whatever side it may come, and ensure that public religious needs be met through the resources of the State.
   62. The Government will maintain the status quo in the
State in matters of religion.

7. Basic Law: The Government,
1968 (Excerpts)

   1. The Government is the executive authority of the
State.
   2. The seat of Government is Jerusalem.
   3. The Government holds office by virtue of the confidence of the Knesset.

4. The Government is collectively responsible to the Knesset.

5. (a) The Government is composed of the Prime Minister and other Ministers.

(b) The Prime Minister shall be a member of the Knesset; any other Minister need not be a member of the Knesset but shall be an Israel national and resident; when a person becomes a Minister whilst serving in one of the offices the holders of which are debarred from being candidates for the Knesset, his service in that office shall cease upon his becoming a Minister.

(c) A Minister shall be appointed to a Ministry but he can be a Minister without Portfolio; one of the Ministers can be Deputy Prime Minister.

6. When a New Government is to be formed, the President of the State, after consultation with representatives of party groups in the Knesset shall place the task of setting up a Government on one of the members of the Knesset who within three days from being asked has informed the President that he is prepared to undertake the task.

7. A period of 21 days to carry out his task is given to the member of the Knesset on whom the President of the State has placed the task of setting up a Government.

8. (In case the member fails, the President may ask another member.)

9. (a) Where the President of the State has not placed the task of setting up a Government under Section 8, or has placed it under that section and the member of the Knesset has not within 21 days informed the President that he is unable to set up a Government, or previously thereto has informed him that he is unable to set up a Government, representatives of parties in the Knesset, the members of which form the majority of the members of the Knesset, may in writing request the President to place the task on a particular member of the Knesset.

11. (If after all these attempts, no government can be formed, new elections are to be held.)

42. Notwithstanding anything contained in any other law, emergency regulations cannot alter this law, suspend its effect, or prescribe conditions thereto; this section is not to be varied except by a majority of the members of the Knesset.

8. Knesset and Local Authorities Elections
(5730) (Financing, Limitation of Expenses,
and Audit), Law 5729 (1969)*

Definitions

1. In this Law:
   "party" means a party named in the First or Second
   Schedule.
   "allocation" means an allocation from the Treasury
   under Section 2.
   "elections" means the elections for the Knesset
   and the local authorities intended to be held
   on the 16th Cheshvan, 5730 (October 28, 1969).
   "election expenses" means expenses for the organization of activities on the party in the election campaign and expenses for propaganda and
   information preparatory to the elections,
   whether oral or written or in any other manner,
   and includes commitments in respect of expenses
   of aforesaid,
   "representatives" means party representatives appointed under Section 5.

Allocation and Apportionment Thereof

2. (a) (1) All the parties enumerated in the First
Schedule shall be allocated out of the Treasury an aggre-
gate amount of 14,400,000 pounds for the financing of election expenses. The apportionment of the said amount among
those parties shall be as set out in the First Schedule.
   (2) The party named in the Second Schedule shall
be allocated out of the Treasury an amount of 180,000
pounds for the financing of election expenses.
   (b) A party which does not, either alone or together with .another party, submit a candidate's list for
the elections to the Seventh Knesset is not entitled to an
allocation, and the amounts of the allocations referred to
in subsection (a) shall be reduced by the amount intended
for it under the First or Second Schedule.

---

*Passed by the Knesset on 1 Adar, 5729 (February 19,
1969) and published in Sefer Ha-Chukkim No. 550, 10 Adar,
5729 (February 28, 1969), p. 48; the Bill and an Explana-
tory Note were published in Hatza'ot Chok No. 807, 5729, p.
54. ($1 = 4.20 Israel Pounds--official rate of exchange,
1972.)

```
                          FIRST SCHEDULE


                     Sections 1 and 2(a)(1)

                                                    Pounds

Alignment (Israel Labour Party, United
   Workers' Party)                                7,440,000
Freedom Movement, Israel Liberal Party
   bloc (Gahal)                                   3,120,000
National Religious Front, Mizrachi, Ha-
   Poel Ha-Mizrachi, and Independents             1,320,000
Independent Liberal Party                           600,000
Tora Judaism, Agudat Yisrael, and
   Religious Independents                           480,000
Israel New Communists                               360,000
Hamahaneh Hatorati, Poalei Agudat
   Yisrael, and Religious Independents              240,000
Ha-Olam Hazeh, Koah Hadash                          120,000
Israel Communist Party and Independents             120,000
Progress and Development                            120,000
Cooperation and Brotherhood                         120,000
Israel Druze                                        120,000
Arab-Jewish Brotherhood                             120,000
Knesset Member, D. Ben Gurion                       120,000

        Total                                    14,400,000



                         SECOND SCHEDULE


                     Sections 1 and 2(a)(2)

                                                    Pounds

Free Centre                                         480,000
```

Limitation of Election Expenses

3. A party shall not incur election expenses to an amount exceeding a total composed of the following two:

(1) The amount of the allocation to which it is entitled under the First or Second Schedule.

(2) An additional amount, not exceeding one-third of the amount of its allocation, out of its own funds.

Transportation of Voters

4.   The transportation on election day, for the purpose of voting, of persons entitled to vote from the area of one inhabited locality to that of another and back, shall be financed out of the Treasury through the Central Election Committee. Such transportation shall be carried out along routes and over distances prescribed by the Central Election Committee, by directions, and in accordance with such procedures and arrangements as it may direct.

Appointment of Representatives

5.   (a) Every party entitled to an allocation shall notify the Chairman of the Knesset, through the representative of its Knesset group, not later than the 17th Av, 5729 (August 1, 1969) of the names of its representatives empowered to act on its behalf for the purposes of this Law. The notification of the appointment of representatives shall be accompanied by their written consent.

(b) The number of representatives shall be not less than two and not more than eight, including at least one who is a Member of the Knesset and at least one whom the party has declared to be familiar with its financial economy and election expenses.

(c) A party has the right to replace its representatives, by notice to the Chairman of the Knesset accompanied by the written consent of the new representatives, provided that the letter include one who is a member of the Knesset and one concerning whom the party has declared as specified in Subsection (b).

Deposit with Chairman of Knesset

6.   Not later than the 27th Elul, 5729 (September 10, 1969), the Treasury shall place at the disposal of the Chairman of the Knesset the amounts of the allocations referred to in Section 2.

Conditions of Payment of Allocation

7. The representatives of every party entitled to an allocation shall furnish the Chairman of the Knesset with the following:

(1) A confirmation by the Chairman of the Central Elections Committee that the party has submitted a candidates' list for the elections to the Seventh Knesset.

(2) A declaration signed by the representatives that the party has made all the necessary arrangements to ensure the keeping of proper accounts of the election expenses, in accordance with the directives of the State Comptroller, including the opening of a special bank account for that purpose; the name of the bank and the number of the account shall be indicated in the declaration.

Advance Payment

8. When the representatives of a party have furnished the Chairman of the Knesset with the documents referred to in Section 7, the Chairman shall transfer to the bank account indicated in the declaration of the representatives an advance payment of an amount equal to 70 percent of the amount of the allocation due to that party under the First or Second Schedule. The advance payment shall not be attachable.

Keeping of Accounts

9. Not later than the 15th Tammuz, 5729 (July 1, 1969), the State Comptroller shall issue directives concerning the keeping of accounts and voucher procedures in connection with the election expenses, and from the 17th Av, 5729 (August 1, 1969), every party entitled to an allocation shall follow those directions and enter all its election expenses, fully and accurately, in a special set of accounts.

Opinion as to Nature of Expenses

10. From the date of publication of this Law in Reshumot to election day, inclusive, every party may apply to the Chairman of the Central Elections Committee, in writing, for an opinion as to whether or not some particular expense is to be regarded as an election expense. The Chairman of Central Elections Committee shall, in consultation with the

Vice Chairmen, give the opinion within one week and shall deliver a copy thereof to the Chairman of the Knesset, the State Comptroller, and the representatives of all the parties entitled to an allocation.

Inspection by State Comptroller

11. (a) The State Comptroller shall inspect the set of accounts referred to in Section 9 and for that purpose shall have all the powers granted him in respect of an inspected body under the State Comptroller Law (Consolidated Version) 5718 (1958).*

(b) The State Comptroller may at any time demand that the representatives shall deliver to him a declaration signed by them concerning facts which, in his opinion, are of importance with regard to the character or nature of some particular expense or to the accuracy of completeness of the entries in the set of accounts of election expenses. A declaration as aforesaid may be made according to the knowledge or the best of the knowledge of the declarants and the Comptroller may, at his discretion, admit it as evidence.

Comptroller's Report

12. (a) Within six weeks of election day, the representatives shall deliver to the State Comptroller their election accounts to the 20th Kislev, 5730 (November 30, 1969), which shall include every election expense the party incurred or became liable to up to that date.

(b) Within ten weeks of the day on which he receives the accounts of any party, the Comptroller shall submit to the Chairman of the Knesset a report of the results of the inspection, indicating:

(1) Whether the party has kept a set of accounts in accordance with his directives.

(2) Whether, according to the accounts, explanations and declarations received by him, he has reached the conclusion that the election expenses of the party were within the limits of the amount permitted under Section 3.

---

*Sefer Hahukkim of 5718, p. 92; LSI (Law Summary of Israel) 12, p. 107.

<u>Payment of Remainder of Allocation</u>

13.   (a) Where according to the State Comptroller's report under Section 12 a party has fulfilled the conditions
set out in paragraphs (1) and (2) of that section, the
Chairman of the Knesset shall transfer to its bank account
the remaining 30 percent of the amount of the allocation
due to it.   This remainder shall not be capable of attach-
ment save for debts arising out of election expenses.
      (b) Where according to the report a party has not
fulfilled the said conditions, it shall not be entitled to
the remainder of the allocation, and the Chairman of the
Knesset shall return the amount which was intended for it
to the Treasury.

<u>Implementation</u>

14.   The Chairman of the Knesset is charged with the
implementation of this Law.

9.   The Party Financing Law, 1973

<u>Definitions</u>

1.   In this Law
      a parliamentary party ("si'ah") is:
            (1) A party which has presented to the Knesset
                elections a list of candidates as a par-
                liamentary party of the previous Knesset
                and is represented in the Knesset by at
                least one Member.
            (2) A party whose representative(s) has/have
                been recognised by the Knesset Committee
                as a parliamentary party.
            (3) A combination of two or more parties main-
                taining a single parliamentary party in
                the Knesset.
      "expenses" are the expenditures of a parliamentary
        party for the organisation of its activities,
        its propaganda and public relations, and the
        maintenance of organisational and ideological
        contact with the public, including commitments
        arising from such expenses.
      "election expenses" are the expenditures specifi-
        cally incurred by a parliamentary party in the
        Knesset election campaign.

147

"current expenses" are parliamentary party expenses, not including election expenses.

"due date" is the 101st day before the Knesset elections, and with regard to elections taking place according to a law for the dissolution of the Knesset, 3rd day after the legislation of that law.

"election period" is the period from the due date to election day.

"finance unit" is a sum determined by the finance committee of the Knesset as a finance unit for the purposes of this law, to be officially gazetted.

The Right to Subsidy

2. (a) Every parliamentary party is entitled under this law:

(1) To the financing of its election expenses during the election period.

(2) To the financing of its current expenses during each month, from the month after the publication of the Knesset election results until the month of publication of results from the following Knesset elections.

(b) The funds for these purposes will be paid by the State Treasury through the Knesset Speaker to the bank account of each parliamentary party.

Calculation of Subsidy

3. (a) The financing of election expenses will be according to one finance unit per seat won by the parliamentary party in the Knesset elections.

(b) The monthly subsidising of current expenses will be five percent of the sum obtained by the party under Subparagraph (a).

Election Expense Payments

4. (a) A parliamentary party that has given the Speaker a letter of confirmation from the Chairman of the Central Election Committee that it has presented a list of candidates for the next Knesset, will be immediately paid an advance on account of the subsidising of its election expenses. The advance will be sixty percent of one finance

unit per Knesset member belonging to the party the day the list of candidates was submitted.

(b) If a party has won at least one seat in the incoming Knesset, it will be paid from the sum accruing to it under Paragraph 3(a):

(1) 85% immediately following publication of election results.

(2) 15% immediately after the State Controller has presented a favourable report to the Knesset Speaker under Paragraph 10(b).

(c) An advance received by a parliamentary party under Subparagraph (a) will be deducted from payments under Subparagraph (b). Should this advance be greater than the sum accruing to the party for election expense financing, the balance will be deducted from the initial sum or from the first payments made to cover current expenses.

7. (a) No party shall spend during the election period for its election expenses more than one-third of a finance unit per Member of Knesset, including local election campaign expenses held at the same time.

(b) No party shall spend during one year more than half the amount accruing to it for current expenditures.

8. No party, either directly or indirectly, shall receive any donation from a legal corporation, including a registered partnership.

9. (a) Each party will keep a set of books according to the directives of the State Controller and will record all income and expenditure.

(b) The books and bank accounts of the party will at all times be available for scrutiny by the State Controller. [Paragraphs 10 and 11 explain this supervision-- Author.]

12. (a) If a parliamentary party is a combination of two or more parties, which together have joint representation in the Knesset, those parties will be considered separate for the purposes of financing current expenditure.

13. Deals with changes in party composition and their relevance to this law.

14. The responsibility of the party to declare true information.

15. Sums paid under this law may not be withheld for any reason.

16. New parties:

Knesset members elected from a list presented by voters--as distinct from a list presented by a party in the outgoing Knesset--will be recognised as a parliamentary party from the first day of the new session.

17. Inapplicability:

(a) This law does not apply to a party which . . .
formally declares its refusal to accept payments under
this law.

(b) This law does not apply to the sums received
by any party by decision of the Histadrut for financing of
its Histadrut election campaign and trade union activities.

18. Voters may be transported to the polls on election
day at government expense . . . under supervision of the
Central Elections Committee.*

10.   The Bader-Ofer Amendment

Knesset Election Law (Amendment No. 4) 1973, approved
by the Knesset on April 4, 1973, Amendment to Article 81.
In Article 81 of the Knesset Election Law of 1969,
instead of Paragraph (d) read as follows:

(d) The seats left over after the distribution
of seats under Paragraph (c) will be divided between the
party lists as follows:

(i) Each list will be assigned a list
quotient by dividing the number of seats won according to
Paragraph (c), plus one.

(ii) The list with the highest quotient
will win one more seat. If two or more lists have equal
quotients, a lottery will be held by the Central Committee
to ascertain the winner of the extra seat.

(iii) Distribution according to (i) and (ii)
will continue until all seats are taken, with the list winning an extra seat according to (i) being reassigned a new
quotient incorporating that new seat.

(iv) A list obtaining no more than half of
all the valid votes won by all lists and having won half
the seats will not participate in further seat distribution
which will continue until completed between all the other
lists.

---

*Translated and abbreviated from the Hebrew text pub-
lished in Sefer Hahukkim, February 1, 1973, No. 680, pp.
52-56.

11. Notice Regarding the Secrecy and Honesty
of the Elections--Elections Law
(Electioneering Methods), 1959

Paragraph 16 of the Elections Law (Electioneering
Methods), 1959, obligates the Chairman of the Central Committee for the Knesset Elections to publish a notice clar-
ifying, for the benefit of voters, their right to a free
vote, to vote as they themselves see fit; and detailing
the instructions contained in the Law for ensuring the
freedom, secrecy, and honesty of voting.

ACCORDINGLY, THE CHAIRMAN OF THE CENTRAL ELECTIONS
COMMITTEE FOR THE EIGHTH KNESSET HAS PUBLISHED THE FOLLOW-
ING NOTICE:

(a) Every voter shall vote for a list of candidates,
in accordance with his own free choice, whether it be the
list whose platform and programme appeal to him, or whether
it be the list whose candidates he would wish to see as
his representatives in the Knesset.

The voter must establish for himself the worth of the
various party platforms, and the capability and suitability
of the candidates of the different parties to manage the
affairs of the country.

(b) Experience has been gained in using election propaganda to influence the voter and to attract him to the
platform and candidates of one party or another--but no
propaganda replaces the voter's obligation to weigh for
himself the question of whether a given party and its candidates really deserve his trust; nor can such propaganda
deprive him of his right to do so. In this connection,
the voter should make a proper distinction between propaganda based on substantive programmes and plans, and empty
propaganda, lacking all positive content.

(c) The Law distinguishes between fit and proper propaganda which is relevant, and which is published or dissemi-
nated publicly (including in circles organised in private
homes) and is not spread secretly, and propaganda which is
objectionable and criminal, e.g., a party trying to spread
its election propaganda through representatives, who, for
example, promise voters that they will obtain them work,
or money, or housing, or any other benefit, if the voter
will vote for the representative's party, and not for
another party. Any party and its representatives indulging
in such propaganda are committing an offense. Such promises are without value--a voter trusting such promises
will find himself deceived and exploited. Furthermore, the

151

law provides for the representatives of a party using such propaganda methods to be imprisoned for a period of five years--and not to be a representative of the people.

This is also the position of a party that sends a representative to threaten any voter that, if he does not vote for his party but for another party, he, the voter, will be dismissed from his employment, or will be evicted from his dwelling, or will be harmed in any other way, or will be denied any benefit due him; such people are also criminals, for whom the law prescribes imprisonment--they should not be voted for by a voter with a conscience, capable of thinking for himself.

(d) No one may require someone else to reveal the list which he intends voting for, or is considering voting for, or which are the lists he does not favour: the elections are secret, and it is every voter's right to keep secret the way he votes--this applying before, at the time of, and after the elections. The Law contains detailed instructions to ensure the secrecy of the elections: the envelope in which the voter places his voting slip is completely closed and cannot be seen through; he may seal it with glue, if he so wishes. The voting booth in which the voter chooses the voting slip of his choice is built and fitted in such a way that no one outside the booth can see him while he is choosing the slip, or when he is putting the slip in the envelope; and no one may be present with him in the voting booth (except in the case of a voter who, because of disease or disablement, is unable to reach the election booth unaided, or cannot make the movements necessary to take an election slip and insert it in an envelope --such persons may take into the booth with them to help them, another person of their own choice). The voter himself places the envelope in the ballot box, and his envelope becomes mixed with the others, so that no one can tell who inserted which envelope.

No one need worry that it is in any way possible, by natural or unnatural means, to find out the list for which he voted. Anyone saying that he has ways or tricks to find out for which list another person voted, or for which lists he did not vote, is lying.

(e) Every citizen has the right to vote in the Knesset elections; he may cast only one vote in the Knesset election. (If he also has the right to vote in the local elections, he may vote in the local elections, at the same time and at a place near the voting booth for the Knesset elections.) Let no one who has already used his right to vote in the Knesset election go to another voting booth to vote a second time--whether he do it by using a forged identity card, or a special card issued to a soldier, or an identity card which is not his.

Anyone who, for the purposes of voting, uses a forged identity card, or an identity card which is not his, or who votes more than once, or who puts more than one envelope in a ballot box, does not only prejudice the honesty of the elections, and their efficacy as a reflection of the wishes of the people; he also exposes himself to the possibility of severe punishment.

(f) A voter who, on election day, is not in the place in which he appears on the voters' list--other than a soldier on active service or an employee of the Israel Defense Forces--may travel, at the expense of the State, to the place where he is to vote: all necessary arrangements have been made for such voters to travel to, and return from the place where they are to vote. All these arrangements have been made so that the citizen entitled to vote will physically be able to use his right, without subjecting him to undue expense. Such journeys are to be made on ordinary bus routes, or on Israel Railways, as the voter decides. These arrangements are not intended to prevent the parties or their representatives from offering voters transport to voting booths, nor is it intended to prevent a voter accepting an offer of transport from a party. But the voter should know that, even if he accepts an invitation from a party, and is given transport to a voting booth, this in no way obligates him to vote for that party; he is free to vote for any other party, in accordance with his free choice.

(g) The right to vote in the Knesset is a right and not an obligation: but if the citizen does not use his right to vote, he does not play the part allocated him by the law of the country, in the democratic process. If we, citizens of Israel, wish to be deserving of this democracy, and to develop and broaden it, let us all make sure we vote in the Knesset elections!

(Haim Cohen, Judge of the Supreme Court, Chairman of the Central Elections Committee for the Eighth Knesset.)

12. Election Propaganda, 1948, 1969, 1973

<u>1948 Election Propaganda</u>

The General Zionists Organization
is
THE CENTRE PARTY

(Advertisement, Palestine <u>Post</u>, December 10, 1948)

WHEN final victory brings peace, the State will need the full constructive support of all its citizens.

Today the State internally suffers from a lack of equilibrium which threatens its social stability.

Labour is powerfully organized; the Collective Sector is favoured by Government which is dominantly Socialistic; public services, including the Civil Service, are subject to effective Leftist pressure.

This growing control of the Left evokes a similar movement from the Right. BOTH DICTATORSHIPS are equally harmful.

In the centre, private, initiative, individual enterprise, small capital, and free professional interests are poorly organized, weak and unprotected. This situation is a menace to future progress.

The General Zionists Organization desires to rally and represent those who are opposed to Left and Right totalitarian control and to assure for them a Fair Deal and Equal Opportunity under democratic rule.

Only a Party which is independent of Left and Right political organs can truly serve the aims of the centre, comprising businessmen, farmers, artisans, manufacturers, liberal professions, officials, and workers, who resent regimentation and believe that individual freedom is essential to a free democratic society.

Support the Centre Party

THE PROGRESSIVE PARTY

(Advertisement, Palestine Post, December 19, 1948)

THE PROGRESSIVE PARTY aspires to implement, in the life of the State of Israel and of the Jewish Nation, the principles of democracy, based on Human Liberty. It inscribes on its banner the ideals of Individual Freedom and of Social Progress; the quintessence of the ideology, moral and social, of the Jewish Prophets and the highest aspirations of the fighters for Right and Liberty in the world at large.

As a member of the World Union of General Zionists, the Party considers itself bound by the principle of giving priority to the aims of Zionism over every other aim. (From the Programme of the Progressive Party.)

Every person who reinforces the PROGRESSIVE PARTY, adds strength to political responsibility and farsightedness, to social cooperation, to the protection of the Freedom of Man, to the advancement of private initiative and cooperative effort, to continuous economic expansion.

JOIN
THE PROGRESSIVE PARTY

HISTORIC FRONTIERS AND CIVIC FREEDOM

(Advertisement excerpts, Palestine Post, December 10, 1948)

TENUAT HAHERUT, The Freedom Movement, the political party which evolved from the Irgun Zvai Leumi, will strive in the purely political sphere to secure the consummation of the aim which the Irgun only partially achieved: the restoration of the whole Hebrew Homeland, east and west of the Jordan. On the immediate situation, Herut regards the early liberation of Western Eretz Israel as not only possible but imperative, and moreover not in conflict with any international undertaking.

There can be no agreement with the invading Arab States until they have withdrawn their armies to within their own borders. From that moment the policy of Israel must be one of peace and constructive friendly relations with its neighbours. As for Abdullah (grandfather of King Hussein of Jordan) there is no room for any agreement with him whatsoever, as he is a usurper in both Western and Eastern Eretz Israel.

The reported negotiations with Abdullah are fraught with the utmost danger. They imply Israeli acquiescence in the presence on its very doorstep not only of Abdullah's soldiers but of Britain, whose retreat from Western Eretz Israel was achieved only at the cost of heavy sacrifice and untold suffering. An agreement leaving Abdullah in control of the Old City of Jerusalem, and of the central triangle means nothing more nor less than the subjection of the State of Israel to the mercy of Bevin, who would confine the Hebrew people in an untenable ghetto, whose disastrous character no grandiloquent name will alter.

Tenuat Haherut is the only true opposition within the State. It is unalterably opposed to the prevailing system whereby the machinery of the State is treated by the various parties as the property of those parties, to be divided up according to the index of strength of each party. This system reduces the official to the servant of his party, and gives rise to the unhealthy practices which now permeate the State service. The basis of the present coalition is purely and simply an agreement on how to divide the spoils. A coalition making for good government can be based only on a POLICY agreement. Tenuat Haherut will itself enter no other kind of coalition and will fight to the uttermost to replace the present system.

WHAT MAPAM STANDS FOR

Excerpts from the Platform of the Party to the
Constitutional Assembly Elections

(Advertisement, Palestine _Post_, December 10, 1948)

1. The State of Israel for the Ingathering of the Diaspora.

Israel will fulfill her national task of liberation for the Jewish people, and her progressive role in the Middle East, by making the Jewish State the territorial centre for the vast majority of Jews.

Immigration into Israel to be Free and Unlimited to the Jews

Immigration is not to be limited to a so called "absorptive capacity" measure of the country. The schemes for absorption must be adapted to the needs and extent of the Aliyah. The working Aliyah creates the absorptive capacity of the country.

Settlement of the Wastelands

The area which will be included in the Jewish State as a result of our military victory and of our political achievements will only really belong to us when covered by a vast network of hundreds of new working and pioneering settlements. Consequently we demand the fullest support and encouragement for the chalutz movements at home and abroad, with autonomy for all forms of settlement on the basis of the right to self-determination by the settlers.

Planned Development of the Country for the Upbuilding of the State

In order to enlarge further the absorptive capacity of the country, to increase its industrial and agricultural production, to raise the standard of living of the people, and to achieve the unification of the country the State must be developed within the framework of a planned and controlled economy. Private initiative will be allowed to function in accordance with the approved development schemes of the State.

2. The State of Israel to be Free of Imperialist Interference.

True independence can be maintained only by absolute opposition to the domination attempts by the imperialist forces. These forces aim at a reduction of our area and attempt to acquire the natural resources of the country for their own benefit and that of their feudal agents. They strive to establish military bases by means of financial and economic subjugation of the people. A stable peace can only be achieved by the full sovereignty of Israel over the whole area from Dan to Akaba; by the liberation of the country from the invading armies; the elimination of the imperialist concessions, and the strengthening of our ties with the progressive forces of the world, with the Soviet Union and the new peoples democracies at their head. ONLY THUS CAN WE INSURE VICTORY, PEACE, AND POLITICAL AND ECONOMIC INDEPENDENCE OF THE STATE.

3. **Alliance with the Arab Peoples for Independence and Development.**

The Arab citizens of Israel will enjoy full civic equality and the right to develop their own language, culture, and religions. Peace-loving Arab refugees allowed to return to Israel on the basis of the peace treaties will be included in the schemes of resettlement and reconstruction. The reunification of the country and the establishment of friendly cooperative relations between the peoples of Palestine will be achieved through economic union between the State of Israel and an independent democratic State in the other part of Palestine. The alliance with the Arab peoples and the strengthening of the progressive forces amongst them will further the liberation of the backward countries of the Middle East from the yoke of feudalism and imperialist exploitation.

9. **Socialist Hegemony in a Progressive Government.**

In this initial period of the State's foundation it is imperative that the Government be built on a basis of a progressive democratic coalition constituted by a united front of the workers' parties within the Histadrut. This united front, based on an agreed programme will determine the conditions under which representatives of progressive democratic non-workers' parties will be invited to participate in the formation of a coalition Government. Only the victory of the revolutionary party of the working class will safeguard the real progressive democratic nature of the coalition and the socialist hegemony in the Government and will prevent surrender to reaction, and clericalism and thereby make possible the uprooting of Fascism.

10. **The Banner of the United Workers Party.**

Gathered around the banner of the United Workers Party towards the election to the Israeli elected Assembly are: all class-conscious workers; all soldiers fighting for the full freedom of their people and homeland, from the oppression of foreign domination; youth imbued with the spirit of chalutziut; all the productive intelligentsia working for a new Socialist society; all the men and women from all walks of life whose fate is bound up with that of the working class.

MAPAI--ISRAEL LABOUR PARTY

Mapai (Mifleget Poale Eretz Israel)--the Israel Labour Party--is Israel's largest political party. At the last General Election in 1965, Mapai polled, together with Achdut Ha'avoda Party (see Ma'arakh), 36.7 percent of the total vote. In the Israel Cabinet, in addition to the Prime Minister, Mr. Levi Eshkol, the following portfolios are held by Mapai Ministers: Agriculture, Defence, Development and Housing, Education, Finance, Foreign Affairs, Justice, Police, Posts and Commerce and Industry.

Mapai gained (together with Ahdut Ha'avoda Party) an absolute majority of 50.9 percent of the votes at the last elections of the Histadrut--Israel Federation of Labour--through which the Party played a vital role in the pre-State period known today as "the State in the making." Imbued with a deep sense of responsibility for every facet of national life, it led the Jewish population politically, socially, economically and in the sphere of self-defence along the difficult path which led to the establishment of the State of Israel in 1948.

Mapai was founded in 1930 through the merger of the two main workers' parties at that time--Hapoel Hatzair and Ahdut Avoda. Since its inception its history has been largely identical with that of the country as a whole, it has taken the initiative in policy and development and been in the forefront of their implementation through times of constant crisis and conflict in the country and unparalleled catastrophe among the Jewish people in the Diaspora. In the spheres of politics and security Mapai took the lead: in determining official Zionist Policy and action throughout the Nazi period in Germany; in reaction to British Mandatory policies towards immigration; in the training and equipment of the "Hagana" to safeguard the security of the Jewish community. Mapai initiated the mobilization of Jewish volunteers from Palestine for service in the Second World War and the formation of the Jewish Brigade, as well as the organisation of the rescue of the Jews from Nazi atrocities, and the organisation of their immigration to Palestine. Mapai representatives headed the delegations which appeared before the Anglo-American and United Nations Commissions of Inquiry and at the United Nations Assembly;

they headed the Jewish national bodies on the declaration of Statehood and were principally responsible for the conduct of the War of Independence against the invading Arab armies.

In the six Knesset elections held during Israel's 16 years of independence, Mapai has held the leading position and has, therefore, shaped the policy of the country insofar as the construction of the new society within it and its social and educational patterns are concerned. The ingathering of the exiles and their speedy integration in the economic, social and cultural life of the country has held a primary place in the activities of the Party.

The security of the country and protection and defence of the borders were tackled in full recognition of the educational part which the Army must play in absorbing citizens of variegated background and origin.

In foreign policy Mapai strives toward peace with the neighbouring countries of the Middle East, and aims at achieving this goal through negotiations with the countries concerned. In general, Mapai believes in pursuing a policy of constructive cooperation with all countries based on mutual recognition of territorial integrity and noninterference in internal affairs according to the principles of the United Nations.

Efforts on an international level to gain recognition for Israel were another significant task inspired by Mapai leadership. Israel was among the first countries of the world to realize her responsibility towards other newly emerging and developing states and has been already even to make sacrifices in order to contribute aid and manpower to those countries in Africa and Asia which ask for and need it.

In striving to stabilize the national economy and at the same time to live by the socialist ideals which are the basis of its existence, Mapai has set a line which encourages the development of every sector of the community in such a way that all contribute to the common good. Large-scale investment and development projects were initiated with a view to increasing production for home supply and export. Agriculture and industry have been expanded so that the country is now self-sufficient in many commodities. Large areas of land have been settled which were previously neglected and barren, especially along the borders and in the Negev, thus simultaneously providing an effective line of settlement outposts. The expansion of industry, cooperatively and government owned was encouraged with a view to closing the gap between Israel's income and expenditure on the one hand and the provision of productive employment on the other.

Both through the media of the Government and of the Histadrut, Mapai has sought to maintain the real value of wages by a policy of progressive taxation, by linking cost-of-living allowances to the cost-of-living index and by introducing a system of production norms and productivity premia in industry.

Mapai's strength may be said to lie principally in the fact that its membership is drawn from every section of the working community of the country: from the collective and cooperative agricultural settlements as well as from individual farmers and farm workers. Tens of thousands of its members are urban workers in industry, transport, mining and other services as well as from the many producers' cooperatives. The two main agricultural settlement bodies are Mapai oriented: Ihud Hakvutzot Vehakibbutzim--United Kibbutz Movement; Tnuat Hamoshavim--Smallholders' Cooperative Settlements. The United Youth Movements of Working and Student Youth--Hanoar Haoved Vehalomed--is identified with the ideological aims of Mapai and has established a number of collective settlements. Mapai members have been elected to key positions in the countrywide trade unions of the Histadrut, thus inspiring and drawing strength and support from every branch and field of constructive endeavour in the country.

In the world Zionist Organisation, Mapai and its associated members of the Ihud Olami (World Union of Zionist Socialist Parties), have 33% of the mandates. The Ihud Olami plays a decisive role in the work of the Jewish Agency and the World Zionist Movement and is a member of the Executive Boards of both these organisations.

The 1960 Council of the Socialist International was held in Israel and Mapai delegates there also showed initiative in the trend within the international socialist movement of branching out from Europe to the new African and Asian States which are seeking new ways in their own development. Mapai is a founder member of the Asian Socialist Conference.

Mapai issues a weekly publication, Hapoel Hatzair, which first appeared in 1907, and Molad, a bimonthly devoted to discussion on subjects of cultural and political interest. Mapai has no Hebrew language daily newspaper and gives its full support to the Histadrut daily Davar, whose editor is a member of Mapai. However the Party publishes newspapers in French (L'Information) and Rumanian (Viata Noastra) as well as two dailies in which the Party

shares ownership with other interests, <u>Letzter Neiyes</u> in
Yiddish and <u>Nowiny-Kurier</u> in Polish.

Mapai also publishes two weeklies, <u>Facla</u>, in Rumanian
and <u>H'et</u>, in Hungarian, and in partnership with others a
Yiddish Language weekly, <u>Illustreite Weltwoch</u>, an English
quarterly <u>Israel Seen from Within</u>, is published in conjunc-
tion with the Ihud Olami, and a monthly bulletin is published in English for distribution.

THE INDEPENDENT LIBERAL PARTY
OF ISRAEL

Political and Social Principles

The following are the principles upon which the I.L.P.
is based.

First and foremost, the security and welfare of Israel,
national unity and interclass cooperation; statehood, ingathering of the Diaspora and integration and absorption
of the newcomers; personal freedom, social justice and
democracy; priority of general interests over partial and
class interests; equal opportunities for all citizens with
no discrimination as to origin, outlook, or class; establishment of Israel as a welfare state; modern technology
in the development of its economy; coexistence of all economic sectors and abolishment of all discrimination or
preference; re-inforcing the Zionist Movement and strengthening the ties between the State and the Diaspora; advancement of Israel's position as a centre of the Jewish people.

The I.L.P. is represented in the Cabinet by Mr. Moshe
Kol, Minister of Tourism, and by M. K. Yehuda Shaari, Deputy Minister of Tourism.

AGUDAT ISRAEL

Election Manifesto of a Religious Party (Full Translation)

(Report of the Fifth World Congress of Agudat Israel,
1964, Jerusalem)

162

With the help of God

The list of the Jews faithful to the Bible, the Israel
Association (Agudat Israel), and non-party religious Jews.

Manifesto

The Agudat Israel Movement which was founded over 50
years ago by the great Biblical scholars and moral leaders
of that generation, is fundamentally a spiritual movement,
as defined in its constituent meeting, and its aim is to
solve all problems arising in the life of the people of
Israel in the light of the Bible and religious law. This
slogan was not particularly original for this has been the
practice of all Israel ever since it stood at the foot of
Mt. Sinai and received the Law, making it a people. The
recent appearance of movements and tendencies in the people
of Israel which believe in other ideas and which reject the
principle of the rule of Biblical law in the people of Israel, have brought about the need for the formation of
Agudat Israel. This compels Agudat Israel to struggle
against the reality of such movements and tendencies, on
various fronts. In the State of Israel, the struggle is
also a political one, and this explains why Agudat Israel
is taking part in the elections to the legislature of the
State, the Knesset, in order to bring the Bible into all
corners of life and to further it in all ways. Agudat Israel has taken upon itself to work according to the instructions of the learned scholars of Bible who are renowned
for their fear of God, and has therefore established a supreme Biblical authority called "The Committee of Great
Biblical Scholars" (Moetset Gedolei Hatorah) to which it is
completely subordinate. In our opinion, it should have
been the first duty of the State of Israel, which has been
founded with God's grace in our Holy Land, to accept the
laws of our Holy Bible as the basis for the entire legal
structure, adjudication, and government operation. Much
to our regret, this has not been done and the delegates of
Agudat Israel will continue to persevere towards the acceptance of this solid basis for all patterns of life in
the State.

The Rule of Biblical Law

The right to take decisions affecting the religion of
our Holy Bible must be and remain the sole prerogative of
(those sensed in) the Bible, which obliges us all, without
drifting left or right.

Education

All levels of education in the State of Israel must
be based on the inculcation of faith in God and his Bible
to all students, without exception, for there is nothing
like faith in God and the observance of His law which can
unite all the tribes of Israel and make them into one people in the land. As we have not yet attained this noble
aim, Agudat Israel has seen it necessary to set up a large
network of original Jewish educational institutions, which
is the crowning glory of our efforts. We shall fight ar-
dently against the present discrimination which harms our
independent schools and shall demand that they be completely
maintained from the State budget. We are sure that religious education shall bring blessings to all. We shall also
fight for the continued existence of veteran institutions
of learning which have guarded the embers of religious
teaching zealously. We see in our Talmudical colleges
(Yeshivot) a firm defense for the spirit of our people, and
in the thousands of scholars who give their entire lives
to the study of the Bible, creators of an aura of sanctity
and purity, and they are therefore eligible for general assistance.

Sabbath

Our holy Sabbath, the soul of Israel, has preserved
our unity and existence through the long years of exile.
We shall not rest until our demand is accepted that there
be a Law for the Sabbath on a national scale which will
make the Sabbath day into a complete holy day of rest for
all residents of Israel, in which everyone will unite with
the Creator and with themselves, a day devoted to eternity.
An end should be put to the granting of permission
to work on the Sabbath in industry by secular bodies. Only
a religious authority may rule what are "matters of life
and death" which allow one to work on a Sabbath or festival.

The Israeli Family

In our tradition the family has always been the centre
of purity and an example for all. One must dam up the
severe breaches which regrettably have appeared of late in
this matter by abolishing all legislation affecting the
purity of the Israeli family (referring to governmental
ordinances recognising existing marriages between Jews and
non-Jews) and by strengthening the authority of Rabbinical
courts in matters of family status.

Any attempt to infringe upon family law as given in the religion of Moses and Israel may divide the nation and (may it never happen), lead to sorrows for generations to come. We shall fight any attempt to recognise "civil marriage" in Israel.

Elimination of the Pig

Bitter experience has taught us that our stand on this issue in the past was right. We demand a Law of the Knesset which will ban pig breeding and the sale of pork and any cheating in this regard must be severely punished.

Pathology

The law of Anatomy and Pathology must be changed in order to stop the terrible practice of post mortems en masse and without need. Our delegates have fought this issue in the past and will continue to do so to prevent tragedies, which have occurred almost daily. We also demand heavy restrictions on archaeology, as the diggers may disturb the dead in their graves.

Religious Services

We shall continue to press for financing by the State of all religious services and institutions. Rabbis must obtain proper salaries while maintaining their complete freedom of decision in matters of religion. Rabbis must be respected and must not become merely government officials.

Social Welfare

Agudat Israel claims credit for the law granting extra pensions for large families from the National Insurance Institute. We shall demand the extension of pension rights to all who are needy, in accordance with Biblical justice.

National Health Insurance

The State must guarantee health insurance to all. We shall fight for a change in the present situation under which the rights of the citizen in matters of health depend on his party affiliation. We shall not agree that health services subsidised by the State should continue to be political tools. Welfare services must be broadened with

increased budgets. Bureaucracy must be reduced and they
should work in a spirit of Jewish benevolence.

War Casualties

Larger pensions should be paid to war casualties, particularly those suffering from the effects of World War II.

Against Anti-religious Coercion

Agudat Israel is very worried by tendencies of anti-
religious coercion which have increased latterly, particularly in new immigrant villages. We demand that immigrant
children be given a religious education. In some villages
jobs are denied to people who do not work on the Sabbath.
This must be stopped.

Foreign Education

The Christian Mission must be banned. It is a national
security risk to be prevented and the government should not
ignore the issue, by allowing mission schools to operate.

Immigration

With the aid of God a million Jews from all corners of
the world have returned to our Holy Land. All immigrants
who want to be absorbed in religious frameworks should be
allowed to do so, for unity will not be attained except
through the Bible. All slums should be dismantled and
their inhabitants given decent housing at easy credit rates.

Settlement

The government should encourage agricultural development, particularly by those farmers who observe Biblical
laws pertaining to agriculture.

The Middle Class

Shopkeepers and artisans should be encouraged, and
their taxation should be lightened. There should be easier
credit facility for them.

Workers and Salaried Employees

A decent standard of living should be guaranteed by
pegging wages to the Cost of Living Index.

Foreign Policy

True to the ideal of peace preached by the Prophets of Israel, the State of Israel must strive for peace with her neighbours and seek friendship with all states.

Israel must cooperate with all elements seeking peace and the strengthening of the UN. Until we reach the Biblical vision of "making swords into ploughshares," Israel must ensure that the Army is well-equipped and trained, and that Biblical Law is strictly observed by the troops, for the spirit of the Bible ensures our moral superiority, over the adversary.

The Israeli Army must continue to be above and beyond all political differences and must enjoy the trust of the entire nation.

Recruitment of Girls

Agudat Israel objects to the recruitment of girls to the Army.

Purification of Everyday Life

We shall strive to purify the atmosphere of Israel, particularly among youth. The way of life accepted today is at variance with our Jewish traditions. Pornographic literature, easy pleasures, corrupt values, and other negative matters are of deep concern, and we shall try to purify the situation by a return to the Bible and its inspiration.

Only by safeguarding the ancient and hallowed traditions of our forefathers can we build our future as a morally health society in our own land.

Structure of Agudat Israel

President: Rabbi Y. Rosenheim
Chairman: Rabbi I. M. Levin
World Executive: 68 members: 33 from Israel
18 from the Americas
17 from Europe

Foreign delegates to the 1964 Congress of the party came from: USA, Canada, Brazil, Argentina, Austria, UK, Belgium, Denmark, France, and Switzerland.

MAKI (Moked) Policy (1969)

Excerpts from "Thesis for the 16th
Congress of the Communist Party of Israel (MAKI)
Communism-Democracy--The Jewish People"

by
M. Sneh
(October, 1968)

For almost fifty years the entire communist movement
regarded national problems including the problems of the
Jewish people, according to Stalin's composition: <u>Marxism
and the National Question</u> (1913), which was accepted as a
kind of fixed theory that should not be questioned . . .
today serious Marxist thinkers challenge Stalin's definition of a nation . . . a serious mistake is the identification of national movements with one class, the bourgeois,
and placing the working class outside the national movements and struggles . . . in general, Stalin's study has
been justly criticized for underestimating the spiritual
motives and elements in the formation and nature of nations.

The Jewish people is the historically created community of people of different classes that was formed by a
number of unifying factors--ethnogenetic, religious, and
national.

The approach of communist theory to the problem of the
Jewish people expressed itself in the unequivocable doctrine that the solution of the problem is the liberation
of the Jew from his Jewishness, that is to say social progress will also bring equality and liberation for the Jewish
citizen (emancipation) and as a result he will assimilate
in the nation in which he lives.

But objective social development in the life of the
Jews did not prefer the trend of assimilation but that of
preserving and strengthening national existence. In recent
times there were three mighty historic events that left
their mark on Jewish life:

(A) The extermination of six of the ten million Jews
     in Europe by Hitlerite Germany.
(B) The establishment of the Jewish State, the State
     of Israel.
(C) The experience accumulated since the October
     Revolution concerning the solution of the Jewish
     problem in the conditions of a socialist regime.

Nothing is more alien to Marxism than the failure to examine theory in the light of practice--in the light of reality that has changed. Let us go therefore and see whether these events confirmed or denied this theory.

Even before the holocaust, anti-Semitism throughout the capitalist world, and especially the anti-Jewish ideology of Hitlerism and the Nuremberg Racial Laws caused the differentiation of the Jews and their isolation (dissimilation). The planned and systematic slaughter of the majority of European Jews naturally increased self-awareness and the solidarity of Jews wherever they may be. Every Jew who remained alive knows and feels that he is alive only by chance--either because he was outside the area of the rule of the Third German Reich or because there wasn't enough time to put him in a gas chamber and furnace. Every Jew knows and feels that he was condemned to death only because of his Jewishness and that only by accident the death sentence wasn't carried out. Every Jew proudly bears in his heart the yellow patch with the Star of David that our brothers were forced to carry on their backs as a sign of disgrace while being still alive, and as a shipping tag to the death camp. To come to this people now and advise them: "Assimilate please, forget that you were Jews, free yourselves from your Jewishness so that you will be free"-- can anything more cynical and cruel be imagined? At any rate it is impossible to give our grieving people such advice in the name of communism; communism came to liberate man from alienation, not to impose it upon him and order him not to be himself.

The establishment of the Jewish state will go down in history as one of dozens of similar events--the establishment of independent states in former colonial countries that liberated themselves by a struggle of peoples for national liberation on the background of the general and deepening crisis of capitalism and the collapse of its colonial system. This correct, rational, scientific definition doesn't express, of course, the impression made by the establishment of the Jewish state on the emotional world of the individual Jew and the historical imagination of all Jews. And no wonder. After all there isn't any precedent in history--not a single instance--of a people establishing its political independence in its ancient homeland after 1,878 years of wandering, persecution, and exile. In any case, the tie of millions of Jews in all parts of the world with Israel was created--and this tie is personal, familial, emotional, religious, and national. The awakening of this approach to the state of the Jewish people among the Jewish minorities in the countries of the world couldn't help strengthening Jewish national consciousness and weakening the tendency of assimilation.

The adaptation of communist theory to the lesson of reality on the question of the Jewish people means to examine the question: what are the national desires of the masses of the Jewish people, the Jewish working class, the popular Jewish strata? and enable these desires to be realised. This is the approach in principle of Marxism-Leninism to national problems: satisfy national needs in order to clear the way for the workers to lead their class struggle for socialism.

Special attention should be granted to the need to cultivate the democratic, progressive, humanistic heritage of Jewish history, culture, and tradition. For a long historic period, religion was the only form to express the spiritual life of the masses of the Jewish people and its best sons. Inasmuch as the Jewish religion is the only religion among the Jewish people, and the Jewish people is the only one that accepted Judaism, a kind of identification has been created between the national and religious concepts. This identification is a matter of the past, but it is impossible to throw out treasures of fine human and national values from the heritage of our past because they were expressed in religious form and have been preserved in religious garb. There are fountains of social, moral and philosophic ideas and values in the ancient religious and modern secular Jewish heritage that can serve as a valuable resource for educating youth and mobilising it for the battles for peace, brotherhood of peoples, national independence, democracy, and socialism.

There are brilliant chapters of struggles for independence and freedom in the history of the Jewish people that can serve as a source of national inspiration and pride to the contemporary progressive Jew from the Maccabean revolt, the war of Judah against Rome, the revolt of Bar Kochba-- to the share of Jews in the revolutionary movements of the last centuries and the October Revolution. The vision of peace between all the nations of the world is the original vision of the ancient Israeli prophets. Values of social justice exist in ancient Israeli law and judicial procedure and powerful expressions of social struggle for the good of the poor, the oppressed and discriminated against are included in the books of the prophets. The commune of the Essenes in Judea almost 2,000 years ago is perhaps the first commune in history. Outside Eretz Israel, too, our people created popular, democratic, humanistic and universal values that infinitely enriched Jewish culture in the Middle Ages and afterwards.

Against the background of the incorrect theoretical position that envisioned Jewish assimilation and the disappearance of the Jews as a people in conditions of progress, serious distortions were--and are--being made in the battle against Zionism. A correct communist relation to a national movement makes an exact distinction between its progressive elements which should be approved and the reactionary which should be rejected. According to this distinction we, too, must examine our relationship to Zionism which is neither more nor less than a national movement.

Stalin's thesis that every national movement is a bourgeois movement even if the proletariat "apparently" participates in it, applied to Zionism, distorted the view of reality. The Zionist movement had a broad national character and included masses from the discriminated against, persecuted and despairing strata of society that regarded immigration to Eretz Israel as their only salvation. The communist approach to Zionism ignored this and also lacked the discernment of the dialectical relationship between the Jewish community in Eretz Israel and British colonialism, in other words, between the Zionist undertaking and the mandatory government. According to the agreement between the Zionist summit and the British government, the mandatory British administration was obligated to help establish the "Jewish National Home." In reality this help was accompanied by severe hindrances and setting the two peoples, Jewish and Arab, against each other, but due to objective circumstances and subjective motives, the Jewish community succeeded in achieving the crystallisation of a nation in the years of the British protectorate over Eretz Israel in spite of all such interference. And here one thing was transformed into its opposite; the Jewish community that was established under the protection of the British Empire came into total conflict with British policy and became a serious factor in the struggle for national liberation (1945-1946). The Jewish people in Israel was one of the main factors in the struggle against colonialism after the Second World War. It caused the British government to leave all of Eretz Israel and thereby played a major role in the battle against imperialism in the Near East.

In the struggle of the communist movement with Zionism, insufficient thought was usually given to differentiate in the Zionist movement between the bourgeois right and the worker-pioneer left in which even a socialist left crystallised that revealed an ideological affinity to Marxism-Leninism.

The communist battle against Zionism also suffered from ignoring the constructive and socialistic-humanistic roles it fulfilled. With all its faults, the Zionist organisation, and especially its worker-pioneer wing, laid the foundation of a Jewish society in the State of Israel.

It goes without saying that the campaign of hate waged at present in a number of socialist states and with the participation of a number of communist parties ostensibly against Zionism but actually against the Jewish people and the State of Israel should be reproved and rebuked. The identification of Zionism with imperialism and the comparison of Zionism with racialism and Nazism are insults to every Jew as a Jew.

1973 Election Propaganda

THE LABOUR ALIGNMENT

Excerpts from the 1973 Election Platform

I. Introduction

1. The elections to the Eighth Knesset will take place after the Yom Kippur War, at the peak of the political struggle for peace, with constant alertness necessary in the face of the risk that the Arab States may be prompted to start the fighting again. The Alignment's programme for the Eighth Knesset must, in all its sections and items, reflect the lessons to be learnt and the conclusions to be drawn from the circumstances and consequences of the war, the preparatory process within nation and society, and the attainment of peace as the cardinal objective.

II. Security

2. The Party Centre applauds the tenacity and triumph of the IDF over the enemy's armies, thanks to its strength and to the heroism of all its ranks. The IDF emerged victorious in spite of the enemy's numerical superiority, his advantage in arms and equipment supplied by the USSR.

3. The Party Centre expresses its sympathy with the sorrowing and the bereaved, its solidarity with the prisoners of war, the wounded, and their kin.

4. Security needs must be foremost among the matters that demand the State's concern, and no effort should be spared to enhance the power and capacity of the IDF, which are the preconditions for the reinforcement of our security and the attainment of peace.

III. Striving Towards Peace

5. The paramount objective of Israel is to attain peace with the neighbouring States and forge bonds of cooperation among the peoples of the region. Since its establishment, Israel has striven to achieve these twin purposes. That it has not yet succeeded is due to the policy of hostility, belligerency, and boycott pursued by the Arab Governments all these years.

6. Today, as well, on the very morrow of a war launched and waged by Egypt and Syria, with other Arab States as their allies, Israel is steadfast in its determination to labour even more perseveringly for the furtherance of peace. In that spirit, the Government has taken several decisions since the outbreak of the Yom Kippur War:

    a. To respond to the cease-fire initiative, and to maintain the cease-fire on a basis of reciprocity;
    b. To sign the Six-Point agreement with Egypt and work for an agreement on the disengagement of forces, and so stabilize the cease-fire;
    c. To express readiness to take part in the peace conference, scheduled for December, 1973.

7. The peace conference is a significant event in the history of the Middle East, and offers the prospect of a radical change in the relations between Israel and the Arab States. It is Israel's wish and hope that the negotiations with its neighbours at the conference will indeed bring about the peace that is longed for.

8. At the conference, and throughout its complex of international exchanges, Israel will exert itself for a peace agreement to be brought about by negotiations—with no preconditions, and without any pressures, or attempts at coercion, from any quarter.

9. The peace agreement for which Israel will contend is one ensuring:

a. Elimination of all manifestations of hostility, blockade and boycott;

b. Defensible boundaries, to guarantee for Israel a capacity of effective defence against military attack or blockade, boundaries based on territorial compromise: those boundaries will replace the cease-fire lines;

c. That Israel shall not return to the lines of 4 June 1967, which were a temptation to aggression;

d. The preservation of Israel's Jewish character, so that its Zionist aims may be realized and its role in aliya and the ingathering of the exiles fulfilled;

4. The opening of a chapter of normal exchanges between Israel and the neighbouring States, in politics, economics, society, and culture.

10. A peace agreement with Jordan will be based on the existence of two independent States, Israel with the unified city of Jerusalem as its capital, and an Arab State east of it. The self-determination of the Palestinian Arabs and of the Jordanians can then find expression in that adjacent Jordanian-Palestinian State, at peace and in good neighbourly relations with Israel. Israel is against the establishment of another separate Arab Palestinian State west of the Jordan.

11. No peace agreement will be signed save with the approval of Government and Knesset.

12. Until a peace agreement is signed, Israel will observe the cease-fire, as well as any interim agreements that may be agreed upon between Israel and its neighbours, as provisional accords on the way to peace.

In the absence of peace treaties or interim agreements, Israel will, as before, undertake full compliance with the situation as it was fixed when the cease-fire came into force.

Israel will take steps to continue settlement and to amplify it, and to set up outposts, in accordance with such decisions as may be adopted by the Government, giving priority to the security considerations of the State.

IV. Relations with the USA

13. Israel prizes the special relations which it maintains with the United States of America and the substantial aid which that country has extended to it. Israel will endeavour to strengthen those relations.

V. Call to World Jewry

14.   Israel, with grateful heart, welcomes the mobilization of the Jewish people all over the world to rally to its side, and calls for their ongoing support in its fight for peace and security, in its strivings to grow stronger in spirit and materially, and in organizing mass aliya.

THE INDEPENDENT LIBERAL PARTY

Excerpts from the 1973 Campaign Platform

Foreign Policy and Defence

In the aftermath of the Yom Kippur War the ILP will strive for a true and lasting peace between Israel and the Arabs--a peace to be based on defensible borders, territorial compromise, and the preservation of the Jewish character of the state.   United Jerusalem will continue to be the capital of Israel.   Peace between us and the Arabs is one of the major aims of Zionism and Israel.   The ILP sees the Geneva Conference as a chance for an historic change in the relations of the two nations who live in the area, and the Government of Israel must make a supreme effort to attain peace while vigorously defending the security needs of the state and the people.

The Jewish people and the State are proud of the Israel Army, which was able to repel a deliberate onslaught of the Arab states and to transfer the battle to enemy territory.   The bravery and sacrifice of the Israeli soldier compensated for what was missing in equipment and prior planning.   The people and state mourn the heavy losses and share the grief of the bereaved families.   The Israel Army must be strengthened in every way open to Israel.   In order to prepare and equip the army for any battle, a formal and binding commitment must be obtained at the highest level of the United States government to supply sophisticated equipment over a long period, in order to prevent the need for renewed approvals or the dispatch of an emergency airlift again.   There must be an end to the signs of politicization which have appeared in the army and which were caused by the Alignment (Maarach) and the Union (Likud).   The politicization of the army endangers its national character. In order to uproot this negative phenomenon, the ILP will propose legislation banning high officers from becoming candidates for party-political posts, unless they have been discharged from the army for at least two years. Israel Army procedures must be scrutinised and supervised by civilians in order to put right severe deficiencies which have come to light. The army must be made more efficient, it should be restored to its rightful position and its moral fibre must be strengthened.

Ever since the 1967 War the ILP has demanded an energetic search for peace and a genuine quest for coexistence with the Arab states. The ILP was opposed to the policy of stagnation and disguised annexation, which were expressed both by the Galili theses (of the Alignment) as well as by the slogan of "not one inch" (attributed to the Union) in demanding that the options for peace be left open. At the same time the ILP was opposed to any withdrawal until a settlement was reached.

The ILP supports the participation of Israel in the Geneva Conference for negotiation with the Arab States in order to reach agreement on peaceful coexistence. After five wars, which we have won, but which have not brought peace, the ILP sees this Conference as a significant development.

The ILP demands that the government should go to Geneva with a sincere desire to reach peace, with readiness to attain an agreement which might bring peace and security to the entire region, while vigilantly and vigorously defending what is vital for Israeli security.

Peace will persist and be firm if it will be just, based on agreed borders which will prevent further wars and which will allow Israel to dwell in safety.

Areas evacuated by Israel under a peace agreement will be demilitarised and no army will be allowed there. There should be arrangements for joint supervision of the demilitarisation.

Steps should be taken to solve the Palestine question, including the refugee problem, by recognising the right of self-determination within the context of a treaty of peace and security with the State of Israel. The ILP believes that the best solution can be found in the framework of a Jordanian-Palestinian state, the regime of which, federative or other, will be determined by its population, which already today is largely Palestinian.

The ILP has long called for permission to be given to the Palestinian Arabs to have a representation, and had this been done years ago, the terrorists would not be able to pose today as the sole spokesmen of the Palestinians. The ILP demands that even at this stage, Arab leaders in Judea and Samaria must be allowed to converse and coalesce in order to become a factor in the peace negotiations.

THE CIVIL RIGHTS MOVEMENT

Excerpts from the 1973 Campaign Platform

The Yom Kippur war has shown that the defective regime harmed not only civil rights and the weaker elements of society but also threatened our very physical security. As we awaken from the past illusions we held regarding our ability to live in tranquillity in the status quo, we must now exhaust all possibilities in reaching a negotiated peace settlement with our neighbours.

The harshness of reality demands the replacement of our existing leadership by new leaders who will enjoy confidence and have the competence to negotiate peace in a spirit of new initiative. Peace treaties must ensure that Israel will have a large Jewish majority in defensible borders, while being aware of the right of the Palestinians to their own self-determination.

While the public is aware of the need to change its leadership, the present electoral system frustrates the likelihood of change. The sovereign right of the citizen to choose his leaders has been handed over to the party machines. The ruling parties have made of the Knesset a rubber stamp in which Ministers do not have to account for the errors and acts of omission and neglect within their areas of responsibility. We shall struggle for electoral reform to ensure a strong bilateral relationship between the voter and his representative.

We shall work for:

--the enactment of a "Basic Law--the Rights of Man and Citizen"--to ensure freedom of speech, conscience, religion, privacy, the right to work, to organise and to move freely.

--the prevention of retroactive legislation.

--legislation compelling the government to inform the public of its actions, plans and debates.

--ensuring the freedom of religion and conscience for every person and group, and for the right to join, or not to join, any religious community or sect.

--the right of every person in Israel to establish a family
without discrimination on grounds of origin, religion or
other existing marriage limitations.
--the full equality of women in the life of the country,
society, the economy, and before the law.
--free education to the age of 18, with the planned growth
of secondary education.
--a fair division of national resources to reduce the gap
between rich and poor. Israel as the State of the Jews offers its citizenship to every Jew in the world. This right
is a basic Zionist concept and cannot be limited by religious criteria. Young Jews around the world should be
encouraged to immigrate, by means of inviting them to par-
take in a human challenge, the construction of a better society.

THE UNION (LIKUD) PARTY

Excerpts from the 1973 Campaign Platform

Foreign Policy and Defence

The right of the Jewish people to the Land of Israel
is inalienable and is combined with its right and aspiration for peace and security. Any suggestion resulting in
the repartition of the Land of Israel--West of the river
Jordan--is rejected a priori. Legal steps must be taken
to extend Israeli sovereignty to the liberated tracts of
the Land. The party will strive ceaselessly for peace with
the Arab States. Peace, after wars, means the signing of
peace treaties to be obtained only by direct negotiations
between the parties concerned. The conditions of peace,
as an indivisible part of the treaty with the Arabs, must
be linked in the light of experience and legality, with
the existence of Israeli control over those areas which in
the past afforded our enemies bases of aggression, and may
yet do so in the future. Massive Jewish settlement in
Judea, Samaria, Gaza, Golan, and Sinai must be given the
highest priority. In the Land of Israel there will be
equal rights for all citizens and inhabitants regardless
of origin, race, nationality, religion, sex, or community.
Any inhabitant of the Land of Israel who requests Israeli
citizenship and accepts the obligation of allegiance to
Israel will receive it. Should he or she prefer to retain

178

a former citizenship, that is permitted. The State will not compel anyone to adopt Israeli nationality.

Israel will contribute to a humanitarian solution of the Arab refugee problem in the way similar problems in other parts of the world, arising from wars, were solved with international aid. Israel will solve the problem of the refugees within her jurisdiction by dismantling the refugee camps and rehabilitating the refugees. The Arab states must solve the problem of those refugees on their territory. The State of Israel was founded in order to realise the dream of the return to Zion, in order that the majority of Jews may return to be concentrated in the homeland. All sons of the Jewish people in Israel and throughout the dispersed Exile share the same fate. There must be a continued national and international effort aimed at the total evacuation of all Jews from Iraq, Syria and other Arab states, to save them from persecution and bring them to safety. The political and public struggle to ensure the free right to immigrate to Israel of the Jews from the Soviet Union is of historical magnitude, to save our brethren and guarantee the future of the Jewish state. Israel, and the Jewish people everywhere, must conduct this battle steadily, around the world. With the aid of enlightened public opinion in the free world we must ensure that every lover of Zion in Russia be allowed to return to the homeland. The proposals of Senator Jackson and Congressman Vanik are vitally important for the sake of free immigration from Russia, which is why the Jewish people and Israel must unhesitatingly support this (American draft) legislation, which enjoys the support of the majorities in both U.S. chambers.

On the 5th of June 1967, when Israel went forth to defend her independence and existence against the aggression of her enemies, the Soviet Union broke off diplomatic relations with her. Should the Russian government initiate and suggest an exchange of Ambassadors with Israel, our country must, before the resumption of diplomatic ties, demand that all Jewish Zionists imprisoned in Russia be released and that all Soviet Jews be permitted forthwith to return to the ancestral homeland. Israeli foreign policy will be governed by the national interest without any social doctrinal consideration. The Land of Israel is part of the free world and will contribute as far as it can to the peace efforts of all nations irrespective of their regime.

Surrounded as we are by enemies, the Israeli army must protect not only the independence but the very existence of the nation. The army must therefore be strengthened in all ways, as the supreme task of the nation. Our security policy will aim to prevent a new large-scale war in the region.

THE NEW COMMUNIST PARTY (RAKAH)

Excerpts from the 1973 Campaign Platform

The NCP stands for peace and security on the basis of UN resolution 242, recognising the sovereignty of Israel and the Arab states, and calling for Israeli withdrawal from all the territories conquered in 1967. The just rights of the Palestinian Arab people must be respected, and Israel must be ensured its freedom of navigation in the Suez Canal and Tiran Straits. The NCP struggles for a foreign policy of peace and neutrality, with friendship for the USSR and other socialist countries. The Soviet Union is dedicated to peace in the Middle East and distinguished between the anti-national policy of the Israeli government and the true national interests of Israel.

The NCP is the revolutionary party of the Israeli working class, and is opposed to a policy which every few years creates wars bringing death and injury to thousands of families.

THE BIBLICAL RELIGIOUS FRONT

(Agudat Yisrael-Poalei Agudat Yisrael)

The Land of Israel was given to us for an inheritance by our Creator and we have never abandoned our rights to it. With God's grace in 1967 we were able to reunify Jerusalem, and the Yom Kippur War again gave us a miraculous victory. So we await daily for our complete deliverance. We shall make peace with our neighbours on the basis of God's promise to His people, strategic necessity, political expediency and international law. We shall defend the Law of God and ensure that a Jew can only be defined according to religious law (halacha). The Jews of Russia and the Arab states must be allowed to immigrate to Israel, poverty must be overcome, and morality in the Biblical tradition must replace corruption, waste, and permissiveness.

THE NATIONAL RELIGIOUS PARTY

Excerpts from Platform Statement, 1973 Elections
(Social Welfare Minister Hazani, in a pre-election speech)

The role of the National Religious Party is to ensure that Israel is not going to become a country with citizens of Jewish origin, but that it remains the Jewish State.

We ask the voter to keep to our traditional Jewish values in these days of trial and confusion, and keep faith with the knowledge that the Almighty will never abandon His people. We want to fortify the spiritual and moral fibre of Israeli society. We oppose extremist policies which will foil from the start any prospect of negotiating a settlement with Israel's neighbours that may lead to peace.

This opposition to political extremism was in keeping with the traditional concept of the NRP's role as a moderating and unifying element in all spheres of national life.

The NRP believes it is in the country's interest to strive for maximum national unity and thus in the Eighth Knesset, the Party will endeavour to bring about the formation of a broad national coalition embracing the main political parties.

The NRP platform refers to three guidelines in peace negotiations: the Jewish people's religious and historic right to the Promised Land; the aspiration for lasting peace; ensuring secure borders. On this threefold premise, the National Religious Party rejects "any programme aimed at sacrificing parts of the Land of Israel, our ancestral heritage, and will never accept such a plan."

Rabbinical Statement on Foreign Policy (1973 Elections)

That All the Peoples of the Earth May Know . . .
(Joshua 4:24)

All this land is ours, absolutely, belonging to all of us; it is nontransferable to others, even in part. "It is an inheritance to us from our forefathers." (Talmud, Tractate Avoda Zara 53,b), as guaranteed by the word of God, whose sovereignty extends over each generation: To our father Avraham: "Unto thy seed will I give this land" (Genesis 12:7), "To thee will I give it and to thy seed forever" (ibid. 13:15), "Arise, walk through the land . . . for unto thee will I give it" (ibid. 13:17), "Unto thy seed have I given this land" (ibid. 15:18), "I will give unto thee and to thy seed . . . all the land" (ibid. 17:8);

181

to our father Isaac: "And to thy seed I will give all these lands" (ibid. 26:3, 4); to our father Jacob: "The land . . . to thee I will give it and to thy seed will I give the land" (ibid. 35:12); to The Children of Israel: "And I will give it to you for a heritage" (Exodus 6:8); "I will give it unto your seed and they shall inherit it forever" (ibid. 32:13).

Therefore, once and for all, it is clear and absolute that there are no "Arab territories" or "Arab lands" here, but only the lands of Israel, the eternal heritage of our forefathers to which others have come and upon which they have built without our permission and in our absence; but we have never abandoned the heritage of our forefathers, nor have we severed our ties with it. We have continually maintained all the bonds of our consciousness with it and the strength of our vehement protest against its cruel and arbitrary occupation by others. Similarly, we have been commanded as to our liberation of it; so we shall never abandon nor sever our connections with it. Also it is known in Arab oral traditions and in their Koran that we are to return in the latter days to our ancestral homeland. This is further confirmed in the proceedings of The League of Nations at the conclusion of the First World War, and in a statement by Lloyd George in my possession, that all this land, to the fullest extent of its Biblical boundaries, belongs under the sovereignty of The People of Israel.

Returning in our times by Divine command to the land of our forefathers, land of our life and of our sanctity, "For the appointed time is come" (Psalms 102:14) and "the end is revealed" (Talmud, Tractate Sanhedrin 98; Kuzari 5:27; Or Hahayim on Leviticus 25:25; Yeshuot Malko Yore Daya, No. 66), we have not wrested any sovereignty from the Arabs who inhabited the land in its desolation, for they had none; rather, we have resettled our land at the collapse of the foreign government that had ruled it temporarily, and with the consent and with the decision of the nations of the world to whom this land had been entrusted for that purpose. Inspired by their cultural enlightenment, they publicly confessed recognition to the righteousness of our sovereign relationship to the land. Also, those Arabs native to the land know and acknowledge the incontestable fact that we have not usurped any governmental control from their hands, as admitted in a document in my possession.

It is common knowledge that we did not drive the Arabs from their settlements here in our ancestral homeland, the land of our prophecy and of our prophets, land of our king-

dom and of our kings, the pinnacle of our Holy Temple and
focus of our influence on all mankind, but rather that they,
of their own accord, whether from exaggerated fears and
self-caused confusion or from political design to spread
distortions, creating "refugee camps" to play upon the
sympathies of the world, both distant and near, fled and
abandoned many of their local settlements. We, on the
other hand, have continued and are continuing to build and
to be built through the awesome wonders of the Lord, Who
from His Temple gives strength and fortitude to His people,
blessed by the Lord, in the holy habour of reconstructing
our nation and our homeland, our Tora and our moral culture,
in righteousness and justice, for the restoration of the
eternal values implicit in our national identity, and for
the reestablishment of the Presence of God and of Israel
in Zion.

"The Lord of Heaven and Earth is with us; the God of
Jacob is our stronghold" (Psalms 46:12). "We shall not
retreat from Thee. Thou shalt bestow upon us as a rebirth
of life and we shall proclaim Thy Will, Lord of Heaven
and Earth, cause Thy Face to shine, and we shall be saved"
(Psalms 80:19, 20).

Rabbi Zvi Yehuda Hacohen Kook
     Son of the Late
Rabbi Avraham Yitzhak Hacohen Kook
First Chief Rabbi of the Holy Land
Jerusalem

APPENDIX D
CHRONOLOGY

CHRONOLOGY

The Ancient Period of Jewish Independence

Before the Common Era

c. 1000 King David establishes his capital in Jerusalem.
c. 960 King Solomon builds the Temple there.
c. 930 Kingdom divided into Judah and Israel.
721   Conquest of Israel by Assyrians.
536   Conquest of Judah by Babylonians; sacking of Jeru-
         salem and destruction of the First Temple.
538-424 Return from Babylon. Building of the Second Tem-
         ple. Persian aid to the Jews.
333   Conquest by Alexander the Great.
323-168 Hellenistic rule.
168-63   Independence under the Maccabees.
63   Jewish kings become vassals of Rome.

Common Era

66   Revolt against Rome.
70   Jerusalem and Second Temple destroyed by Rome.
73   Last stand of Jewish rebels at Masada.

Foreign Rulers

132-135 Revolt of Bar Kochba against Rome, in Galilee.
352   Second Jewish revolt in Galilee.
395-638 Byzantine rule.
614   Persian-Jewish attack on Byzantium.
636   Arab invasion.
1072   Seljuk invasion.
1099   Crusader invasion.
1291   Mamluk invasion.
1517   Ottoman invasion.
1799   Napoleonic invasion.

The Return to Zion

1878	Petach Tiqva, first pioneering village, founded.
1895	Herzl publishes The Jewish State.
1897	First "Jewish Parliament"--the Zionist Congress--meets in Basle.
1904	Jewish labor movement founded.
1909	Tel Aviv city founded.
1911	Degania, first collective village, founded.
1917	British Army defeats Ottomans, captures Jerusalem.
1920	Histadrut (General Federation of Labour) founded.

The Mandatory Period: The Embryo State

1922	League of Nations confirms Mandate for Jewish National Home with U.S. endorsement.
1925	Hebrew University opened in Jerusalem.
1939- 1945	Six million Jews massacred by Nazis in Europe.
1947	United Nations resolves to establish Jewish State.

Independent Israel

May 14, 1948	Declaration of Independence.
May 15, 1948	Arab states invade Israel and are defeated.
January 25, 1949	First Knesset elections.
March 10, 1949	First cabinet formed, responsible to the Knesset. Prime Minister: David Ben Gurion.
May 11, 1949	Israel admitted to the United Nations.
January 26, 1954	Moshe Sharett becomes prime minister.
November 3, 1955	Ben Gurion again prime minister.
October 29, 1956	Israeli-Egyptian War. Sinai occupied, subsequently evacuated.
December 8, 1961	Israel joins GATT (General Agreement on Trade and Tariffs).
June 26, 1963	Levi Eshkol becomes prime minister.
June 4, 1964	Israel signs trade agreement with European Common Market.
August 30, 1966	New Knesset building inaugurated in Jerusalem.
May 23, 1967	Egypt closes Straits of Tiran, challenges Israel's existence.
June 5-10, 1967	Israel defeats Egypt, Jordan, Syria, Iraq.
March 17, 1969	Golda Meir becomes prime minister.
October 6, 1973	Syria and Egypt attack Israel and are repulsed.

December 31, 1973	Eighth Knesset elections.
Early 1974	Geneva Peace Conference seeks Middle East peace.
March 10, 1974	Golda Meir forms postwar cabinet.
April 11, 1974	Golda Meir resigns.

COMPOSITION OF THE NEW ISRAELI CABINET

On June 3, 1974, a new cabinet was formed by the former Ambassador of Israel to the United States, Yitzhak Rabin, with a narrow majority in the Knesset.

The breakdown (by party and bloc membership) is as follows:

Labour Movement

Prime Minister: Yitzhak Rabin (Mapai, but with strong personal ties to Ahdut Ha'avoda)

Deputy Prime Minister and Minister for Foreign Affairs: Yigal Allon (Ahdut Ha'avoda)

Minister without Portfolio: Israel Galili (Ahdut Ha'avoda)

Minister of Agriculture: Aharon Uzam (Mapai)

Minister of Labour: Moshe Baram (Mapai)

Minister of Commerce and Industry: Haim Bar Lev (Mapai)

Minister of Police and Interior: Shlomo Hillel (Mapai)

Minister of Education and Culture: Aharon Yadlin (Mapai)

Minister of Information: Aharon Yariv (Mapai)

Minister of Justice and Religious Affairs: Haim Yosef Zadok (Mapai)

Minister of Housing: Abraham Offer (Mapai)

Minister of Finance: Yehoshua Rabinowitz (Mapai)

Minister of Health and Social Welfare: Victor Shemtov (Mapam)

Minister of Immigrant Absorption: Shlomo Rosen (Mapam)

Minister of Transport: Gad Yaakobi (Rafi)

Minister of Defense: Shimon Peres (Rafi)

Liberal Movement

Minister of Tourism: Moshe Kol (ILP)

Minister without Portfolio: Gideon Hausner (ILP)

Minister without Portfolio: Shulamit Aloni (CRM)

Minister of Communications: not yet assigned

MAIN ELEMENTS OF POLICY

Excerpts from Speech by Prime Minister
Yitzhak Rabin, June 3, 1974

A. To safeguard Israel's security, to foster
the strength and power of the Israel Defense
Forces, and to strive constantly and persistently
for a true peace.
B. To build a modern, just, free and independent
society living a dynamic and culturally rich life
in a stable democratic system, with every effort
to involve the younger generation in decisions
and responsibility.
C. To ensure social welfare through the application of a special effort by the community for the
advancement of those strata still in distress.
D. To increase immigration and improve absorption methods in the effort to stimulate tens of
thousands of Jews from all countries of the
Diaspora to settle in Israel; a constant endeavour
to forge closer ties with World Jewry.
E. To make incessant efforts to consolidate and
develop the economy.
F. To strengthen our international position and
the establishment of closer relationships with
the nations of the world, first and foremost with
the United States.

The aspiration for peace has guided and will continue
to guide the policy of the government. Twenty-six years
of war have not in any way altered our view of peace with
our neighbours as a central goal of our policy. In the
future we will continue to strive to reveal every hope and
every spark of hope for the advancement of peace. Our policy is clear. We prefer peace to new military victories,
a stable peace, a just peace, an honourable peace, but not
peace at any price.
The Six Day War gave the State of Israel the greatest
military victory in Jewish history.
But we were not intoxicated by victory. The Government of Israel was ready to attain a peace agreement with
our neighbours being prepared for territorial compromise.
But this readiness met with no response. Under no
circumstances will the Government of Israel agree that
threats of war, international pressure and terrorist activ-

ity shall compel us to return to the situation and the conditions which existed before the Six Day War.

Two obstacles were raised by the Arab states on the road to peace:

A. The demand for an Israeli commitment to total withdrawal to the lines of 4 June 1967 as a pre-condition for any dialogue.

B. Opposition to all direct negotiations between the parties at every stage of negotiations.

The Yom Kippur War has brought about a change in this attitude of our neighbours and only this change has made it possible to achieve the separation of forces agreements.

Israel's Relations with Jordan

We shall be prepared to discuss with the government of Jordan the problems between us. We are interested in concluding peace negotiations with Jordan. We aim at a peace treaty with Jordan which will be founded on the existence of two independent states: Israel with united Jerusalem as its capital and an Arab state to the east of Israel. In the neighbouring Jordanian-Palestinian state, the independent identity of the Palestinian and Jordanian Arabs can find expression in peace and good neighbourliness with Israel. Israel rejects the establishment of a further separate Arab state west of the Jordan River.

During the discussions on the establishment of the outgoing government, the question arose how the government should act if, after negotiations with Jordan, the hour of decision should arrive. The answer to this question was clear: the government would conduct negotiations with Jordan and take decisions at each stage of the negotiations but no peace treaty would be concluded with Jordan if it involved territorial concessions involving parts of Judea and Samaria before the people were consulted in new elections. This undertaking is also given by the new government.

Membership in the Geneva Conference

In this connection I must note that the new government will maintain the policy of those participating in it. This Conference was arranged for the holding of negotiations between the states directly involved in the question of peace in the Middle East--Egypt, Syria, Jordan and Lebanon --which border on Israel. Should it be proposed to invite any other body such a proposal, like any other raised within the framework of the Conference would require the prior approval of all the states which have agreed to participate in the Conference.

Israel rejects the invitation of representatives from the sabotage and terror organizations as participants or observers. The Government of Israel will not conduct negotiations with terrorist organizations whose declared goal is the destruction of the State of Israel.

Israel's Relations with the United States and the Jewish People

Over the last few years the friendly relations between Israel and the United States, its presidents, leaders and peoples have grown firmer and stronger.

Now after attainment of the separation of forces agreements with Egypt and Syria there are grounds for believing that the United States will increase its substantive aid to Israel. The friendly relations between us and the U.S. and the interests common to both our countries have not prevented us in the past nor will they prevent us in future from meticulous insistence on positions vital to Israel's survival and development, even if our positions are not acceptable to the United States.

The Jewish people in the Diaspora have been and will always be the State of Israel's truest ally. The Government will work to strengthen the ties between the Diaspora and Israel. We shall try to encourage Jews abroad to be involved in the experience of Israel. We shall seek ways to have them share in our thinking about the momentous problems which need to be resolved and to facilitate their investment of spiritual and not only material resources in Israel.

SELECTED BIBLIOGRAPHY

BOOKS

Arazi, A. <u>Ideological Change in Israel</u>. Cleveland: Press of Case Western Reserve University, 1968.

_____. <u>Le Systeme Electoral Israelien</u>. Geneva: Droz, 1963.

Curtis, M., and M. Chertoff. <u>Israel: Social Structure and Change</u>. New Brunswick: Transaction Books, 1973.

Deshen, S. <u>Immigrant Voters in Israel</u>. Manchester: Manchester University Press, 1970.

Dror, Y., and E. Gutmann, eds. <u>The Government of Israel</u>. Jerusalem: Hebrew University, 1964.

Elon, A. <u>The Israelis, Founders and Sons</u>. London: Sphere Books, 1972.

Etzioni, A. <u>Alternative Ways to Democracy--The Example of Israel</u>. Jerusalem: Hebrew University, 1966.

Fein, L. J. <u>Politics in Israel</u>. Boston: Little, Brown and Co., 1967.

Freudenheim, Y. <u>Government in Israel</u>. Dobbs Ferry, N.Y.: Oceana Publications.

Lissak, M., and E. Gutmann. <u>Political Institutions and Processes in Israel</u>. Jerusalem: Hebrew University, 1971.

Ministry for Foreign Affairs, Information Division. <u>Facts About Israel</u>. (Annual.) Jerusalem: Keter Books, 1973.

Ministry of Education. <u>Israel Government Yearbook</u>. (Annual.) Jerusalem: Central Office of Information, 1970-71.

Ministry of Interior. <u>Election Results</u>. Jerusalem: Central Bureau of Statistics, 1969.

Rosetti, M. The Knesset, Its Origin, Forms and Procedures.
Jerusalem: Government Printing Press, 1966.

Seligman, L. B. Leadership in a New Nation--Political Development in Israel. New York: Atherton Press, 1964.

Zidon, A. Knesset--The Parliament of Israel. New York:
Herzl Press, 1967.

ARTICLES

Akzin, B. "The Knesset." The International Social Science
Journal 13 (1961): 567-582.

_____. "The Role of Parties in Israeli Democracy."
Journal of Politics 17 (1955): 545-587.

Arian, A. "Electoral Choice in a Dominant Party System."
In The Elections in Israel--1969. Jerusalem: Jerusalem Academic Press, 1972.

_____. "Split-Ticket Voting in Israel." Western Polit-
ical Quarterly 20 (1967): 373-383.

_____. "Voting and Ideology in Israel." Midwest Jour-
nal of Political Science 10 (1966): 265-285.

Avineri, S. "The Sources of Israeli Socialism." Israel
Horizons 19, no. 3 (March 1971): 25-26.

Czudnowsky, M. H. "Legislative Recruitment under Proportional Representation in Israel, a Model and Case
Study." Midwest Journal of Political Science 14
(1970): 216-248.

Lazar, D. "Israel's Political Structure and Social Issues."
The Jewish Journal of Sociology 15, no. 1 (June 1973):
23-44.

Witkon, A. "Elections in Israel." Israel Law Review 1
(1970): 42-52.

THE PRESS

The Jerusalem <u>Post</u>, <u>Haaretz</u>, and <u>Maariv</u> have been used extensively in preparing this book. In addition, much political material may be gleaned from the following party newspapers:

<u>Davar</u>	Histadrut, generally pro-Mapai
<u>Hamodia</u>	Agudat Yisrael
<u>Hatzofeh</u>	National Religious Party
<u>Al Hamishmar</u>	Mapam
<u>Kol Haam</u>	Communist

Two party newspapers are no longer published, but their files are of historical value.

<u>Lamerhav</u>	Ahdut Ha'avoda
<u>Haboker</u>	General Zionists

The opposition Likud Party has no paper of its own but is often able to present its views through Ha'aretz.

ABOUT THE AUTHOR

DAVID M. ZOHAR is Consul for Information at the Consulate-General of Israel in Los Angeles, and has served at Israeli diplomatic posts in Kathmandu, Nepal; Bombay, India; and Washington, D.C.

Mr. Zohar was educated at the Hebrew University, Jerusalem, and the University of Bombay, India.

RELATED TITLES
Published by
Praeger Special Studies

CRISIS DECISION-MAKING: Israel's Experience
in 1967 and 1973
                    Abraham R. Wagner

THE ROLE OF COMMUNICATIONS IN THE MIDDLE EAST
CONFLICT: Ideological and Religious Aspects
                    Yonah Alexander

ISRAEL AND IRAN: Bilateral Relationships and Effect on
the Indian Ocean Basin
                    Robert B. Reppa, Sr.

ISRAEL'S DEVELOPMENT COOPERATION WITH AFRICA, ASIA, AND
LATIN AMERICA
                    Shimeon Amir
                    foreword by Abba Eban

MIDDLE EAST OIL AND U.S. FOREIGN POLICY
                    Shoshana Klebanoff

DATE DUE

NOV 2 6 1981		
SEP 7 1989		
SEP 2 1 1989		
APR 0 5 1999		

HIGHSMITH 45-220   PRINTED IN U.S.A.

DATE DUE

NOV 2 6 1981			
SEP 7 1989			
SEP 2 1 1989			
APR 0 5 1999			

HIGHSMITH 45-220   PRINTED IN U.S.A.